MODERN

AFGHANISTAN

DISCARD

IRAN

ARGENTINA

IRAQ

AUSTRALIA

IRELAND

AUSTRIA

ISRAEL

BAHRAIN

ITALY

BERMUDA

JAPAN

BOLIVIA

KAZAKHSTAN

BRAZIL

KENYA

CANADA

KUWAIT

CHINA

MEXICO

COSTA RICA

THE NETHERLANDS

CROATIA

NEW ZEALAND

CUBA

NIGERIA

EGYPT

NORTH KOREA

ENGLAND

NORWAY

ETHIOPIA

PAKISTAN

FRANCE

PERU

REPUBLIC OF GEORGIA

RUSSIA

GERMANY

SAUDI ARABIA

GHANA

SCOTLAND

GUATEMALA

SOUTH AFRICA

ICELAND

SOUTH KOREA

INDIA

UKRAINE

MODERN WORLD NATIONS

Japan

Charles F. Gritzner
South Dakota State University

Douglas A. Phillips

Kristi L. Desaulniers

CHELSEA HOUSE
PUBLISHERS
A Haights Cross Communications Company

Philadelphia

Frontispiece: Flag of Japan

Cover: View of Mount Fuji.

CHELSEA HOUSE PUBLISHERS

VP, NEW PRODUCT DEVELOPMENT Sally Cheney
DIRECTOR OF PRODUCTION Kim Shinners
CREATIVE MANAGER Takeshi Takahashi
MANUFACTURING MANAGER Diann Grasse

Staff for JAPAN

EXECUTIVE EDITOR Lee Marcott
PRODUCTION ASSISTANT Megan Emery
PICTURE RESEARCHER 21st Century Publishing and Communications, Inc.
COVER DESIGNER Keith Trego
SERIES DESIGNER Takeshi Takahashi
LAYOUT 21st Century Publishing and Communications, Inc.

A Haights Cross Communications ✦ Company

http://www.chelseahouse.com

First Printing

1 3 5 7 9 8 6 4 2

Library of Congress Cataloging-in-Publication Data

Gritzner, Charles F.
  Japan / Charles F. Gritzner, Douglas A. Phillips, Kristi L.
Desaulniers.
     p. cm. — (Modern world nations)
Includes index.
  ISBN 0-7910-7239-8 (hardcover) — ISBN 0-7910-7504-4 (paperback) 1.
Japan—Juvenile literature. [1. Japan.] I. Phillips, Douglas A. II.
Desaulniers, Kristi L. III. Title. IV. Series.
  DS806.G75 2003
  952—dc21
                              2003009309

ISBN 0-7910-7239-8

Table of Contents

Japan

Bonsai is an aspect of Japanese culture that illustrates the harmony between humankind, nature, order, and beauty. These dwarf trees are prized for their longevity and beauty.

1

Introducing Japan

It is one of the most amazing countries in the world. The Japanese call it *Nippon* or *Nihon*, meaning the source of the Sun. Others call it the Land of the Rising Sun. We call it Japan. This small nation of scattered islands off the eastern coast of mainland Asia is often called the "Miracle of the Orient." It has risen from obscurity and self-imposed isolation to a position as a global economic giant in little more than a century. Yet considering the country's physical geography, its history, and its huge population, Japan should have been a huge failure. Japan had to overcome many seemingly insurmountable obstacles to achieve its present-day place among major world nations. The Japanese peoples' spirit, determination, work ethic, and knowledge have been their primary tools in achieving this "miracle."

Japan poses many questions. How has such a small country,

with almost no natural resources, become the world's second strongest industrial economy? How can people with traditions so different than those of Americans still be like us in so many ways? How did a country that attacked the United States during World War II and suffered the devastating consequences of its actions become one of our strongest allies? Why has Japan's economy weakened during recent years? What is its future in these troubled economic times? These are just some of the intriguing questions that will be answered in the pages of this book.

The Japanese place a high value on the harmony between humankind, nature, order, and beauty. One trait associated with Japanese culture (way of life) that illustrates these values is the *bonsai* tradition. A bonsai is a "dwarf" tree, often with gnarled trunk and of great age. Such trees are grown in small, shallow pots and with little soil. Yet they thrive and are prized for their durability and beauty. The bonsai tradition and technique, which involves extensive pruning of growth, was first practiced in China. It appears to have been introduced into Japan during the Kamakura period, about 800 years ago. The Japanese rapidly adopted the method. In a short time, they far surpassed the Chinese in the quality and beauty of bonsai trees. In translation, an ancient Japanese scroll says, "To appreciate and find pleasure in curiously curved potted trees is to love deformity." Understanding the bonsai tradition provides some lessons that help us better understand Japan and its people.

The bonsai tradition, for example, is ancient and many of the trees are very old. Japanese culture is also ancient and today, Japanese people enjoy the world's longest life expectancy. Bonsai are rugged in appearance. So is the country of Japan, with its several thousand islands dominated by rugged mountain landscapes. Bonsai trees are small, gnarled, and grow in very limited space and soil. The first impression of many travelers to Japan is how small and crowded things are. Japanese houses, by American standards, are tiny, as are vehicles, appliances, and even the people themselves, many of whom are quite small in stature. The country's 127 million people are crowded into a very small area, as are bonsai in their tiny pots. And like the bonsai with its limited amount of soil, the country has almost no natural resources to help its economy grow.

When China introduced the bonsai tradition, the Japanese rapidly adopted the technique and improved the practice. In a similar manner, when the West introduced industry, commerce, and urbanization, the Japanese rapidly adopted the new ideas. Within slightly more than a century, they became the world's second ranking industrial power. Japan also quickly became urbanized. Today, Japan's capital city of Tokyo, with Yokohoma and other adjoining suburbs, forms the world's largest metropolitan center with a population of nearly 30 million.

Even the "deformity" of the bonsai trees has a parallel with Japan and its people. Japan, perhaps more than any other country, suffers from deformities of nature. They come in the form of frequent and often devastating earthquakes, volcanic eruptions, tropical storms, floods, and other natural hazards. Finally, bonsai trees are things of great beauty. As you journey through Japan in the pages of this book, the authors hope you will come to see the beauty of Japan. To see the geographic beauty radiated by this unique land and its enduring people.

Mount Fuji, Japan's highest mountain, is located on the island of Honshu. The beauty of its snowcapped peak has inspired Japanese artists for centuries.

2

The Natural Environment

I n many ways, nature has not treated Japan kindly. In fact, few countries face more geographical and environmental obstacles than does Japan. Its location off the eastern edge of Asia isolates the country from the rest of the world. Japan faces the challenge of extreme fragmentation. The archipelago, or chain of islands, includes four major islands—Hokkaido, Honshu, Shikoku, and Kyushu—and thousands of smaller ones (3,413 by one count!). To further complicate its geographical distribution, the islands lie scattered along a southwest-northeast axis spanning nearly 3,000 miles (4,800 kilometers). Providing transportation among the islands is difficult and costly. Fragmented countries often suffer from conflicting cultures and can be very difficult to govern.

The natural environment also poses many economic challenges.

It offers few natural resources to support the country's huge industrial economy. Approximately 95 percent of all environmental resources (metals, fuels, wood, and so forth) used in Japan's booming industries must be imported. Additionally, because of its rugged terrain, only about 15 percent of Japan's land is relatively flat and well suited to farming, urban development, and transportation. The country also experiences many natural hazards. In fact, few countries on Earth are more subject to nature's wrath than is Japan. In this chapter, you learn about these obstacles and how the Japanese have adapted to them.

LOCATION

Location is often the most important of all environmental conditions. Certainly, this holds true for Japan. The country's location holds the key to understanding much of its history and geography. Huge and powerful China lies some 500 miles (800 kilometers) to the west, across the East China Sea and Sea of Japan. Russia's vast Siberian territory looms less than 200 miles (320 kilometers) across the Sea of Japan. Only a few miles separate South Korea from the Japanese islands. The Communist-controlled and often belligerent "Hermit Kingdom" of North Korea lies about 500 miles (800 kilometers) across the Sea of Japan. To the east, across some 4,000 miles (6,400 kilometers) of open Pacific Ocean, lie Japan's major markets in the United States and Canada.

Island countries, if they are to progress, must overcome the challenge of being isolated from other lands, peoples, ideas, and economies. To solve this problem, the Japanese have developed one of the world's best networks of sea and air linkages. For travel between islands they have created one of the world's finest domestic air, rail, and water (ferry, bridge, and tunnel) networks. "Getting around" poses little problem for most Japanese. An island location can also

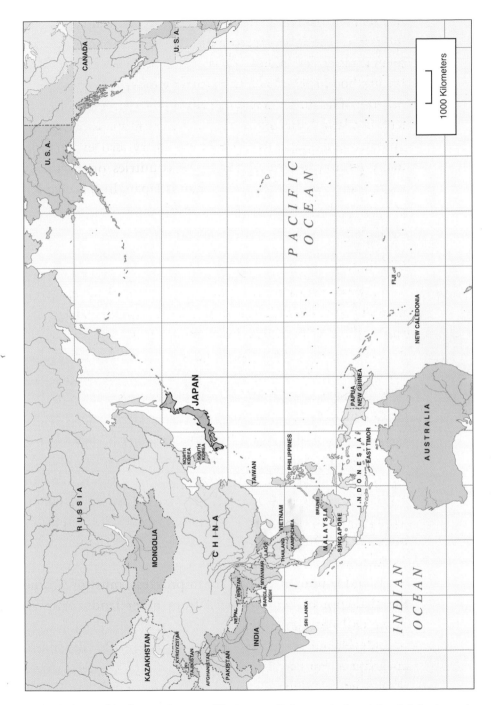

Japan is located in the northern Pacific Ocean off the coast of mainland Asia. Japan's island location has both protected and isolated the country throughout history.

benefit a country. Isolation, for example, has been a chief factor in preserving the unity of Japanese people and culture. Until the United States and its allies successfully invaded Japan in 1945, bringing an end to World War II, no conquering army had ever reached Japan's shores.

A true appreciation of Japan's location is difficult to gain from looking at a flat map. If Japan is viewed on a globe, however, the importance of the country's position relative to other nations can be better understood. Japan lies just beyond Alaska along what geographers call a "great circle route" between North and South America and much of eastern Asia. To see this relationship, place one end of a string anyplace on the Americas and the other end crossing coastal China, the Philippines, Singapore, or Indonesia. No matter where the ends are placed, the string will fall on or close to Japan. As the focus of global trade and commerce has changed from the North Atlantic to countries bordering the Pacific Rim, Japan's location has become a great asset. To the west, in southern, southeastern, and eastern Asia live more than half of the world's people (and rapidly growing potential markets). The world's largest markets, the United States and Canada, are separated from Japan by about a 10-day voyage by huge, fast, cargo ships or a half-day flight by cargo plane.

LAND

Volcanic mountaintops that rise from the bottom of the Pacific Ocean form nearly all of Japan. Slightly more than 80 percent of the country is composed of rugged hills and mountains. In fact, only about 15 percent of Japan's land is classified as plains. The lack of plains makes travel, farming, and building difficult and costly. Because most of the country's huge, sprawling cities are located on plains, much of the flat land is not available for farming. With few exceptions, Japanese settlement, agriculture, and industry have avoided the mountainous regions. Many such areas remain sparsely populated, quite isolated, and economically underdeveloped. The small valleys of flat land and narrow coastal plains support much of Japan's population and economy. Indeed, few places in the world can match Japan for crowded space.

Of Japan's several hundred volcanoes, none is more picturesque, widely recognized, or worshiped by its people than is the beautiful Mount Fuji (also called Fujiyama or Fuji San). In fact, it is one of Japan's most widely recognized symbols. This famous, cone-shaped, extinct volcanic peak towers 12,388 feet (3,776 meters) above the Kanto Plain about 70 miles (110 kilometers) southwest of Tokyo and Yokohama.

Japan's land features have posed many challenges. As you will learn later in this chapter, Japan's land also can be deadly. The threat of volcanic eruptions is only one of the natural hazards with which Japanese must contend; there are also earthquakes and various kinds of earth flows and slides.

WEATHER AND CLIMATE

Climate is defined as the long-term average of daily weather conditions. Meteorologists (scientists who study the atmosphere) and climatologists (scientists who study the weather) are interested in such atmospheric elements as temperature, precipitation, wind, and storms. Japan lies in the middle latitudes. The southernmost island of Okinawa is located at 26° North Latitude, the same as Miami, Florida. Northern Hokkaido reaches about 46° North Latitude, comparable to central Maine. Because of this latitudinal span, Japan has a wide range of climates similar to that of the eastern coast of the United States. Most of Japan located south of Tokyo enjoys a mild, humid subtropical climate similar to that of the coastal southeastern United States. To the north, a more moderate climate prevails, with cooler

Japan is composed of four main islands — Hokkaido, Honshu, Shikoku, and Kyushu —
and thousands of smaller islands. Japan's capital and largest city, Tokyo, is located
on the island of Honshu.

summers and longer colder winters similar to those of New England.

Japan's temperatures are influenced by latitude, closeness to the sea, and elevation. Latitude determines the angle at which the rays of the sun strike Earth's surface. Heating is greatest in the equatorial latitudes and decreases toward the poles. Southern Japan, therefore, enjoys a warm climate and long growing season. Temperatures generally decrease as one goes northward. Tokyo, in central Honshu, has a climate similar to that of coastal North Carolina or Virginia. Farther northward, Hokkaido's temperatures are similar to those of the northeastern United States. Because of its cold, snowy winters, Hokkaido has hosted the Winter Olympics twice.

No place in Japan is located more than 100 miles (160 kilometers) from the sea. Indeed, closeness to the ocean plays an important role in moderating the country's temperatures. Land temperatures near large water bodies generally do not get as hot or cold as do those in places located away from large water bodies. In Japan, temperatures rarely reach 100°F (38°C). In the south, Shikoku, Kyushu, the Ryukyu Islands, and southern Honshu enjoy a mild, humid subtropical climate. At lower elevations, frost is uncommon. Here, farmers enjoy a 365-day growing season and are able to produce two rice crops each year. In the north, winter temperatures do not get as cold as they do at comparable latitudes in the United States.

Finally, much of Japan is mountainous. Elevation exerts a strong influence on temperatures. In Japan, a person can be sweltering in a lowland location, yet look upward at snow-covered mountain peak such as the summit of Mount Fuji. Typically, temperatures drop about 3.5°F (about 1°C) with every 1,000 foot (300 meters) increase in elevation. With about 80 percent of Japan covered by hills and mountains, elevation is an important temperature control.

Rainfall is abundant throughout Japan. Amounts of rainfall range from more than 80 inches (200 centimeters) in much of the south, to about 20 inches (50 centimeters) in drier portions of Hokkaido. In lower elevations of central and southern Japan, nearly all moisture falls in the form of rain. In the far north and at high elevations on the island of Honshu, winter precipitation often falls as snow, sometimes very heavy. As is true throughout most of the world, summer is the season of heaviest precipitation. Particularly in central and southern parts of the country, summer storms—including those associated with typhoons (Pacific Ocean hurricanes)— can bring torrential rain, severe flooding, landslides, and mud flows.

Precipitation in Japan is affected by a system of seasonal monsoon winds. These winds blow onto the continent during the summer and out of the continent's interior during the winter. The seasonally shifting winds also cause a change in precipitation patterns. During the winter months, winds blowing out of Asia sweep across the Sea of Japan bringing moisture to the western-facing mountain slopes. During the summer, the winds shift direction, blowing from the east and bringing more moisture to eastern Japan. No place in Japan, however, suffers from prolonged seasonal drought.

ECOSYSTEMS

At one time, forests covered most hillsides in Japan. Forests of evergreens and broadleaf deciduous trees thrived in the warm, humid south. Northern Honshu supported forests consisting of cone-bearing evergreens and broadleaf deciduous species. Dense forests of cone-bearing evergreens also covered much of the cooler northern island of Hokkaido.

Nearly all housing in Japan, and much of the fuel burned in traditional homes, comes from wood. At one time, the country's forests were severely depleted. Today, however, much of the woodland has been restored. Rather than cutting

Fishing traps help provide seafood, which is one of the staples of the Japanese diet. These fishing traps at Arai, a settlement south of Tokyo, are located close to shore.

its own forests, Japan has become the world's leading importer of lumber and other forest products (including sawdust used in the making of pressed board).

Japan's marine ecosystem is vital to its survival. The country has long depended on the ocean for food. The waters surrounding Japan are among the world's richest fisheries. Fish, shellfish, crustaceans, and even edible seaweed abound. Japanese fishing vessels also ply the world's seas in search of catches. Indeed, the Japanese diet consists mostly of seafood. Some scientists believe that diet is one reason the Japanese enjoy the world's longest life expectancy.

ENVIRONMENTAL HAZARDS

Few places can match Japan in terms of environmental hazards. The country has experienced some of nature's most violent events, including earthquakes, volcanic eruptions, tsunamis ("tidal waves"), typhoons (hurricane-like storms), earth flow or slide, and flooding. Additionally, various areas of the country are subject to less devastating hazards. Hokkaido, for example, frequently suffers from raging summer forest fires and blinding winter blizzards. Because the country and its people are constantly threatened by nature's wrath, Japan is the world leader in natural hazard research, prediction, and protection.

Japan is located in a region of geologic instability known as the "Pacific Ring of Fire." This region includes approximately 80 percent of the world's volcanoes and is subject to frequent earthquakes. Japan is a world leader in the occurrence of both environmental hazards. Additionally, violent events occurring on the ocean floor can cause devastating tsunamis, incorrectly called "tidal waves."

Geologically, nearly all of Japan is a result of volcanism. That is to say, nearly all of the country's land has risen from the seafloor as a result of volcanic activity. In fact, Japan is home to about 100 active volcanoes, some of which erupt with great regularity. Many other volcanoes are classified as being inactive, or dormant. Scientists believe that the country's most famous volcano, Mount Fuji, is dormant. In recent history, none of the country's volcanoes have erupted with devastating results. People have adjusted to the threats posed by the volcanoes. Settlement and land use are designed to minimize potential destruction caused by periodic eruptions.

Few places on Earth are more prone to earthquakes than is Japan. In fact, the country averages about 1,500 earthquakes each year—about four each day! Nearly all Japanese, no matter where they reside, live in constant threat of tremors. In addition to the direct destruction caused by earthquakes, they also trigger other hazards, including crushing landslides and crashing coastal tsunamis. During the 20th century, the country experienced 13 major earthquakes measuring 7.0 or higher on the Richter Scale (a measure of earthquake intensity). Such earthquakes can be devastating, particularly if they occur in a densely populated area.

Japan's most disastrous earthquake in terms of loss of life happened just before noon on September 1, 1923. The violent tremor struck near the heart of the country's most densely populated area—the Kanto Plain, home to the huge cities of Tokyo and Yokohama. Its magnitude of 8.3 on the Richter Scale was comparable to that of the 1906 earthquake that devastated San Francisco, California. The event left Tokyo's business, industrial, and residential districts in ruins. Because the earthquake struck around noon, many homes and restaurants had fires lighted to prepare lunch. Traditional Japanese homes, made mostly of wood and paper, provided abundant fuel for the hungry flames. No water was available to fight the raging inferno, because water pipes were broken by the tremor. As many as 140,000 people died and hundreds of thousands were left homeless in the Great Tokyo Earthquake. This tragic event remains Japan's greatest natural disaster as measured by loss of human life.

Another terrible earthquake struck Japan in the early dawn of January 17, 1995. At that time, most residents of Kobe—Japan's fifth-largest city with a population of 1.5 million—were yawning and stretching themselves awake. Suddenly, disaster struck. In a mere 20 seconds, a huge earthquake (7.2 on the Richter Scale) rocked Kobe to its very foundation, leaving

Earthquakes are a persistent danger in Japan. In 1995, a major earthquake struck the city of Kobe, killing more than 5,000 people and leaving over 300,000 people homeless.

much of the city a blazing ruin of tangled destruction. More than 5,000 lives were lost and another 37,000 people were seriously injured. Nearly 200,000 buildings were ruined and an estimated 300,000 people (one-fifth of the city's residents) were left homeless. Because pipelines ruptured, nearly 1 million households were without water or natural gas. Property losses were estimated to be as high as $100 billion, making it the world's most costly natural disaster of all time. Ironically, Kobe was considered to be one of Japan's safest cities in terms of potential seismic activity and damage.

Tsunamis (Japanese for "harbor wave") are huge waves caused by earthquakes that occur on the ocean floor. No place on Earth is more prone to tsunami devastation than is Japan—with its many cities and towns built bordering the sea on low-lying coastal plains. At sea, a tsunami can pass unnoticed as nothing more than a swell traveling at a speed of up to 500 miles per hour (800 kilometers per hour). As a tsunami approaches the shore and shallow water, however, the water rises and begins to crest in a series of huge waves. Under certain conditions—as in a funnel-shaped harbor—a tsunami can rise to more than 100 feet (30 meters). The surging waves destroy everything in their path as they crash ashore, then carry debris back to sea with the receding water.

With much of its population clustered along the coast—and particularly around harbors—Japan is extremely vulnerable to tsunamis. In 1792, a tsunami killed about 15,000 people in Shimabara, a coastal city in western Kyushu. Over the years, the Japanese have become the world leaders in studying, predicting, and protecting against this potentially devastating environmental hazard.

ATMOSPHERIC HAZARDS

Japan is subject to many atmospheric hazards, including floods and blizzards. The most devastating atmospheric hazards, however, are typhoons. (Pacific typhoons are a type of storm similar to Atlantic Ocean hurricanes.)

Typhoons are huge storm systems that can measure hundreds of miles (kilometers) across, with winds, clouds, and rain stretching even farther out from the "eye," or storm center. The storms begin over the warm tropical waters of the Pacific Ocean and drift in a westerly to northwesterly direction. Because the islands of Japan lie along a general southwest to northeast axis, they fall directly across the path of many such storms. In fact, during an average year about 30 typhoons pass through this part of the Pacific Basin, some of which strike Japan.

The often ferocious storms bring raging winds that exceed 75 miles per hour (120 kilometers per hour) and can reach 150 miles per hour (250 kilometers per hour). Japanese homes, built of wood and other light materials, are no match for winds of this speed. Wind damage, particularly along the coast, can be severe. Water associated with the storms poses an even greater threat than the wind. Immediately along the coast, winds can create a huge wall of water that crashes ashore destroying everything in its path. Inland, torrential rains associated with the storms can cause severe flooding as water rushes down steep mountain slopes. Moreover, water-saturated earth frequently gives way, creating mudflows or landslides that can bury everything in their path.

ENVIRONMENTAL POLLUTION

As Japan's population grew and its economy changed from agriculture to industry, much of the country's natural environment suffered. Beautiful natural landscapes were destroyed as the land became overcrowded with people and settlements. Expanding industrial development also damaged the land. During the 20th century, the country experienced numerous disasters caused by environmental pollution. In some places, industrial wastes contaminated the soil, toxic dust and smoke polluted the air, and sewage poisoned the streams.

Even the sea became poisoned. Beginning in the 1950s, hundreds of people living near Minamata Bay on the island of Kyushu became ill. They began to suffer a severe breakdown of the central nervous system. Eventually, some 3,000 people contracted the "Minamata disease," and hundreds of children were born with birth defects. In 1959, scientists discovered the cause. For decades, a chemical company had been dumping mercury waste directly into the bay. Marine life in the bay consumed the mercury which, in turn, was passed on to humans who caught and ate the fish.

By the 1960s, the Japanese people began to recognize the devastation caused by pollution and other forms of environmental damage. They began taking steps to conserve and protect their environment. Today, Japan has some of the world's strictest regulations protecting the environment.

The Jomon (today's Ainu) were the first inhabitants of the Japanese islands. Today, most of the few remaining Ainu live on the island of Hokkaido, the northernmost of the four major islands of Japan.

3

Japan's Early History

The hermit crab is a very practical creature. It wanders the sea floor in search of a suitable shell it can occupy for protection. Occasionally, it leaves the shell to search for food, but slips quickly back into its shelter when danger approaches. For much of its history, Japan has been much like the hermit crab. It has remained secluded and avoided contact with outsiders. However, modern Japan has become a successful partner in the world community. Japan's history can help shed light on these conflicting traditions.

Most archaeologists (scientists who study early humans) believe that the islands of Japan were first inhabited about 20,000 to 30,000 years ago. These early settlers were called the Jomon. Historians believe that the Jomon were the ancestors of the Ainu who still exist in small numbers on the island of Hokkaido. The Jomon were related to peoples in southeastern Asia and were a hunting, fishing, and gathering culture. They were nomadic and existed primarily along the coastlines in Honshu and Kyushu, where they roamed following food sources.

THE FIRST DYNASTY

It was during the Jomon era that Emperor Jimmu started the Yamato dynasty. According to legend, Emperor Jimmu was a direct descendent of the Sun Goddess. Until World War II, Japan's emperors claimed roots extending back to Jimmu and the Sun Goddess. This divine right to rule existed for nearly 1,500 years. Today, the emperor still plays an important social role in Japanese society, although he no longer has political power.

Around 300 B.C., the Yayoi people replaced the Jomon. The Yayoi were from Southeast China and most likely left the mainland because they were fleeing the Chinese Han military. The name "Yayoi" comes from the area in Tokyo where archaeologists first discovered artifacts from this culture. The Yayoi fled China through Korea and settled in Japan where they mixed with the existing Jomon peoples. The Yayoi were not nomadic. Rather, they introduced and developed agriculture in various areas that were suitable to farming. With so much mountainous land, farmland was limited. But at the time, so was Japan's population. Many small communities based on farming developed during this era. Most importantly, rice became a major crop during the Yayoi period.

The Kofun era followed the Yayoi. It is also known as the Yamato period. It began around 300 A.D. and lasted until 710 A.D. During the Kofun era, people built massive earth and stone tombs. The people came from China and Korea, bringing with them an advanced way of life and technology. They developed advanced social and political institutions. They also introduced Chinese and Korean cultural traditions to the islands. Some scattered Kofun settlements developed into small kingdoms. During this time, certain clans (groups of families) began to gain power. The most powerful of these clans was the Yamato.

During the Kofun era, the Koreans introduced the Chinese written language. Japan underwent other significant changes during this time. Yamato leaders developed new political institutions, created new social classes, and introduced Buddhism as the official religion. The area around Nara and Osaka blossomed into a center of political power with the rising fortunes of the Yamato clan. Most of Japan felt the influence of China and Korea. The Ainu people, however, remained separate. Eventually they moved northward to Hokkaido to distance themselves from the other cultures that were influencing Japan.

THE NARA PERIOD

During the Nara era (710-794 A.D.), Chinese culture continued to influence Japan. Chinese became the language of business and government. A new religion, Confucianism, was introduced from China. The Japanese built a new imperial capital in Heijokyo (present-day Nara). This was Japan's first permanent capital, and the Japanese modeled it after the Chinese capital. Nara soon became a powerful city with nearly 200,000 people, many of whom worked in government. The new government produced coins and collected taxes from farmers. In time, the imperial government tightened its grip on the people. This led to warfare as various members of the imperial family and other leading families fought for power and influence. Other problems arose as farmers could not pay their taxes and began to lose their lands. This caused a shortage of tax money, which caused the government to reduce its military strength. Decreased military strength, in turn, led to the formation of local armies. All of these factors led to a decline of Nara's imperial rule.

In an effort to regain control, Japan's rulers moved the capital from Nara to Nagaoka in 793. One year later, government leaders moved the capital again, this time to Heiankyo, a city whose name means "capital of peace and tranquility." Eventually the name was shorted to Heian. Heian later became the modern city of Kyoto. Heian, like Nara, was modeled after Chinese capitals. This city served as the imperial capital of Japan for over 1,000 years until the Meiji restoration moved the seat of government to Tokyo in 1868. The Heian era saw great advancements in literature, art, and religion. The Fujiwara family controlled the imperial court and was highly influential during this era. Through strategic marriages, they developed broad political control that reached a pinnacle of power under Regent Fujiwara Michinaga around 1016. Eventually, their reach extended too far. They were unable to manage the distant regions, which often felt neglected. Thus, some families were allowed to possess large land estates in an effort to relieve the central government of its obligations to outlying regions. At the same time, these upper-class landowners gained political and economic power.

Decline of the Heian period started when problems arose, such as corruption among local officials. With the central government in decline, local clans started to advance their own military efforts. These developments were designed to bring about more control at the local level. Unfortunately, once these armies formed, the local clans started fighting among themselves in what has been called the Gempei Wars (1180–1185). The wars were essentially battles to establish supremacy. Eventually, two families—the Taira and the Minamoto—fought for dominance. A key naval battle occurred in the Shimonoseki Straits in 1185. In the Battle of Dannoura, the Minamoto leader Yoritomo defeated the Taira. This was a turning point in the Gempei Wars and marked the end of the Heian era.

THE FIRST SHOGUNS

In about 1192, Yoritomo assumed leadership and became Japan's first shogun. A shogun is a hereditary title given to military commanders. Frequently, the shoguns operated as the real power behind the emperor. This form of government was known as a shogunate. Yoritomo was the first shogun in the

Minamoto Yoritomo became the first shogun in 1192 A.D. after defeating the Taira clan. Yoritomo was a ruthless leader who killed anyone who threatened his power — even members of his own family.

Kamakura era, so named because Yoritomo established his political center in the city of Kamakura. The Kamakura era lasted nearly 150 years, from 1185 until 1333. In the beginning, Yorimoto quickly moved to eliminate his enemies. He eliminated individuals who had been his allies during the war. He even killed two of his brothers, both of whom had assisted him during the war. To make sure that his brothers' families would not challenge him, he even had their infant sons killed! Thus, the Kamakura era started in a bloodbath, a tragic pattern that continued through much of this era.

Some positive things also occurred during the Kamakura period. Government leaders developed a currency system that helped local businesses thrive. This was also the era of the samurai, the hereditary warrior class who served as the military in a feudalistic system established by Yoritomo. The samurai lived in the castle of a daimyo (local leader), and were paid when they were called into battle. Unlike mercenary soldiers paid to fight for anyone, the samurai lived by a strict code of honor called *bushido*, which demanded that they remain eternally loyal to their daimyo.

Trade increased during this time and, unlike European feudalism, farmers could own their own land. In the late 13th century, the Japanese repelled invasion attempts by Kublai Khan, the great Mongol ruler of China. Although Khan's forces had superior weapons, the fierce samurai warriors and severe weather conditions helped the Japanese prevail. The good fortune of bad weather happened in 1274 and again 1281. Typhoons forced the Mongols to retreat from their sea attack. Because these typhoons saved Japan from invasion, the Japanese called them *kamikaze* (divine winds). Much later, during World War II, Japanese suicide pilots were called kamikaze fighters, because they were asked to repel the invasion of Japan.

After the wars with Kublai Khan, the central government was left with few resources. Thus, it was unable to reward the samurai and local daimyo who had helped to defend Japan. This caused unrest and eventually led to the end of the Kamakura period around 1333.

STRUGGLES FOR POWER

The demise of the brutal Kamakura shogun leadership left a vacuum that was briefly filled by Emperor Go-Daigo. He was older, wiser, and more able to exert his leadership over the shogun than were emperors during the Kamakura era. He defeated all of the remaining Kamakura leaders except one, Shogun Ashikaga Takauji, who had established a rival dynasty with his own emperor in a capital near Kyoto. Thus, there were two competing imperial courts. In time, however, Ashikaga became ruler of all Japan.

Ashikaga ushered in the Muromachi period in Japan's history, so named because he set up his capital in Muromachi, an area near Kyoto. He passed the title of shogun onto his son and thus the hereditary line of the family was established for the Muromachi era. This era was marked by less centralized power than under the Kamakura and by the rising power of the daimyo, which means "great names." Most of the daimyo were military men who had accumulated power, samurai, land, and wealth.

The daimyo passed on their riches and influence to only one male, rather than dividing it between all their children. This was strategic, because it kept power consolidated in one family. Family estates, wealth, and power were not broken up as had been done in the past. Women continued to have very little influence or power and could not become daimyo. The practice of not breaking up estates caused great battles within families. Under this system, jealousy often took hold. Family members sometimes killed the chosen male heirs so that some-one more favorable to them would become the next daimyo.

Because of the decentralized rule during the Muromachi period, the daimyos accumulated great amounts of land and power. Market economies developed in many areas controlled by the daimyos. In these early markets, business people sold agricultural products, clothing, sandals, and other basic needs to people living in an area controlled by a daimyo. People usually bartered or traded for goods, but during this time coins also became a common way of paying for market goods. Many of these business people became very wealthy during this time. Their new wealth gave them greater power and political influence.

Deterioration of central authority and the rising power of the daimyo and local business people divided Japan in the late 15th century. A series of battles, known as the Onin War (1467–1477), took place mostly near Kyoto. Fighting continued for more than 100 years as coalitions between different daimyos came together and fell apart. No one was strong enough to unite Japan during the early 1500s.

ARRIVAL OF EUROPEANS

In the 1540s, the Portuguese arrived in Japan. They brought two important things to Japan: firearms and Christianity. The introduction of firearms increased the technology available to warring factions in Japan and made killing easier. Those daimyo who were able to secure these new weapons rapidly gained superiority over rivals who only had traditional weapons. After the arrival of the Europeans, more years of bloody conflict followed and thousands of people died in fighting.

In the 1560s, a daimyo named Oda Nobunaga tried to unite and bring Japan under his leadership. Before Nobunaga could accomplish this goal, however, he was assassinated. His death and those of other strong leaders caused a continuing power struggle until Tokugawa Ieyasu seized control in 1603. This started the era that historians call the Tokugawa, or Edo, period. Edo is the early name for Tokyo. Tokugawa Ieyasu moved the capital to Tokyo in the early 1600s. To control the daimyo, the Tokugawa shoguns required that all daimyo spend half of the year in Tokyo and half on their estate. In Tokyo, the central government could keep an eye on these local leaders. Spies were used to gather information and root out traitors.

The government also viewed Christians as a threat. The first Christian missionary, Francis Xavier, arrived in Japan in 1549. He and other missionaries convinced some soldiers and other Japanese people to convert to Christianity. Ieyasu felt threatened by both the foreign and Japanese Christians. Ieyasu banned Christianity in 1614 and implemented a number of strategies to eliminate the religion from Japan. He ordered Christians to give up their faith or leave the country. Those who remained were persecuted, and many were killed. In 1638, over 35,000 Japanese Christians gathered in a fort to make a courageous last stand against their oppressors. Ieyasu's army, in a merciless battle, killed most of the Christians. Only about 100 survived.

With Christianity virtually eliminated in Japan, the Tokugawa shoguns closed Japan's doors to European trade and other contact. There was only one exception to complete isolation from European influences. The Japanese permitted the Dutch to conduct some trade, but only with small ships that were limited to the port of Nagasaki. Other European ships were attacked if they tried to enter Japanese harbors. China and Korea were permitted to conduct limited trading, but only in small ships. Japanese people were not allowed to travel to other countries. Japanese rulers banned books and other foreign items that could spread European ideas.

With the door firmly closed to most Europeans, Japan became much like a hermit crab hidden in its protective shell. For centuries, the shell had been the waters surrounding Japan. The sea had provided a natural defense that helped to keep out most outsiders. For nearly 200 years more, this shell would be used to protect Japan from the outside world. Thus, for over two centuries under the Tokugawa shoguns, Japan was an isolated country. Isolation played a very important role in determining Japan's future.

The Japanese navy destroyed much of the Russian fleet during the Russo-Japanese War (1904–1906). This marked the first time a modern European power had been defeated in war by an Asian country.

4

The Birth of Modern Japan

Japan's policy of isolation during the Tokugawa era protected the country against outside threats. During the mid-1850s, however, it became apparent that Japan's closed door also kept out technology and other useful new ideas. Japan was falling far behind the Western industrialized world.

In 1853, American naval officer Commodore Matthew C. Perry sailed into Tokyo harbor with battleships. His ships were steam-powered, made of iron, and had powerful cannons. The Americans also had new and better rifles. Japan still relied upon old technology that was now quite harmless against these new advances in military weaponry. Perry wanted Japan to open its doors to foreign trade. Because of the American's superior weaponry, the Japanese were forced to agree to Perry's terms. They were intimidated and realized that they could not compete against the powerful American battleships. Thus, the door to Japan was pried open.

JAPAN OPENS ITS DOORS

After years of seclusion and isolation, the arrival of the Americans and Europeans threw Japan into political turmoil. Many Japanese wanted to resist the intrusion of outsiders. In 1867, they restored power to the emperor. The ruler who came to power was only 15 years old. His name was Emperor Mutsuhito and his rule initiated the Meiji era. Meiji means "enlightened rule," something that Japan desperately needed at that time. After centuries of division and fighting, the era of the shoguns had ended. A courageous and enlightened young emperor would determine Japan's future.

Early in 1868, the youthful Mutsuhito called nearly 400 leaders to the Imperial palace. He pledged to them that he would take Japan in a new direction. These pledges are known as the Charter Oath. In the document, Mutsuhito said that Japan would develop its economy and seek knowledge from around the world. These and other progressive statements in the Charter Oath threw open the doors of Japan to the outer world. This was a startling reversal of the policies of the closed-door era. New leaders emerged with revolutionary new ideas as Japan threw off the shackles of isolation. Feudalism and class social structures were eliminated. Compulsory education was introduced, requiring all Japanese youngsters to attend school. Telegraph lines and trains were introduced. Japan built a new and modern navy and renegotiated its treaties with the United States. In 1889, Japan adopted a new constitution patterned after that of Germany. In it, the emperor granted more freedom to the people. The Meiji Restoration brought enormous changes to Japan.

Some Japanese opposed these radical changes. In 1877, a shogun led nearly 40,000 troops against the government in the Satsuma Rebellion. The shogun was fighting to preserve his power. The rebellion, however, met with crushing defeat. In the battle, Meiji soldiers killed thousands of the rebel samurai. The traditional power of the samurai and shoguns was broken forever.

The Meiji era was truly a time of great changes. With the new centralization of power, great opportunity existed for rapid advancement. Introduction of new military technology and other knowledge from the West led to a rapid modernization of Japan's military forces. While the new constitution of 1889 provided for a Diet, or legislature, the lower house was elected by only a small portion of the population. This meant that the military and a few traditional leaders still held great power. This factor would later cause problems for Japan.

During the mid-1800s, the United States and other Western powers had pressured Japan into signing unfair treaties. To become a world power, Japan had to renegotiate these treaties and make them more fair. Japanese leaders also understood that their country needed a strong economy and military in order to become a major world power. This was Japan's goal at the beginning of the Meiji Restoration. By the 1890s, the country reached its goal and had become a great world power.

JAPAN AS A WORLD POWER

During the late 19th century, most of the world's powerful nations were scrambling to gain colonies. Possessing colonies enabled these nations to obtain natural resources from their foreign territories and then sell manufactured goods back to the colonists. Imperialism (gaining control of foreign lands) was an important element of foreign policy for many nations. Japan decided to participate in this global economic and political strategy. Japan thought that it could gain control of many important natural resources by extending its power to China. Japan had very few resources and it needed metals, fuels, and other resources to support its economy. Foreign territories under Japanese control also could provide markets for Japanese manufactured goods.

By the turn of the 20th century, Japan had emerged as a military and manufacturing power. The Japanese government supported corporations and strong ties developed between business and government. Japan developed successful transportation systems modeled on those of Western nations. The Japanese people embraced foreign ideas and adapted their culture to help the country move forward. Japan had moved from isolation to welcoming many important ideas from the West. As a result, it developed quickly in both political and economic terms.

Japan established its place on the international stage through war. In 1894, Japan went to war with China and won some territory. Then, in 1904, Japan declared war on Russia. Japan had established itself as a major world power that had to be respected. Its war against Russia marked the first time that an Asian country had defeated a modern European power. Strong military leadership and modern military technology helped the Japanese win. With these impressive victories under their belt, Japanese leaders moved to secure additional natural resources and colonies.

In 1910, Japan annexed Korea. The Japanese military was far stronger than that of Korea. In fact, Japan was able to seize Korea simply by threatening to use force. Japanese occupation of Korea lasted until 1945 and created a strong resentment of Japan by the Koreans that still lingers today. About this same time, Japan increased its control of the island of Taiwan. These strategic moves into Korea and Taiwan increased Japan's appetite for a still-larger empire. This ambition for more territory eventually led Japan into conflict.

In the early 20th century, relations between Japan and the United States worsened. In 1905, President Theodore

Roosevelt hosted a peace treaty meeting in Portsmouth, New Hampshire that ended the war between Japan and Russia. The Japanese complained that their country had not received all that it should have because of pressure from the United States. In the United States, anti-Japanese sentiments increased as the fear of Japanese aggression heightened mistrust. Under Roosevelt, the United States also strengthened its presence in the Pacific with a naval base at Pearl Harbor in Hawaii. All of these activities increased the tensions between the United States and Japan.

World War I (1914–1918) benefited Japan in some ways. Western nations were too busy with the war to conduct trade. This gave Japan the opportunity to form trade links with other Asian countries. Japan's economy flourished during this time. However, major problems struck Japan when the war ended. Economic deflation damaged the economy as prices dropped. Moreover, shortages of rice, Japan's primary food, caused widespread rioting. By the early 1920s, Japan was at a crossroads.

MILITARY RULE

In 1926, Hirohito became emperor of Japan. Historians call this era the Showa Period, meaning "enlightened peace." During Hirohito's early years, the military became increasingly frustrated with democratic rule by civilians. They believed that the military budget was not being increased fast enough. They also thought that the military would be more effective than civilians in running the government. Civilians, the military reasoned, were too preoccupied with domestic issues, such as the economy. Some military officers wanted to return more power to the emperor. Other officers, however, believed that they would be more effective as rulers if the emperor held only a symbolic role. In 1930, the civilian government signed a peace agreement with the United States and European nations. This agreement was short-lived, however, because Japanese military officers did not really want peace.

In 1931, the Japanese military seized control of Manchuria, a region in northeastern China. By 1932, Japan had established a puppet government in Manchuria, renaming the region Manchukuo. The international community, including the League of Nations, was furious. When Japan's civilian leader, Premier Inukai Tsuyoshi, criticized the military actions in Manchuria, he was assassinated. This tragic event marked the start of unquestioned military authority in Japan. All domestic dissent was silenced. The military was clearly in control.

Japan continued to expand its power throughout Asia. In 1937, Japan invaded China and was involved in the horrible plunder of several Chinese cities. In the city of Nanking, for example, Japanese soldiers murdered hundreds of thousands of innocent civilians. Japanese troops raped and tortured many women and children. This brutal treatment of conquered people continued in other areas into which the Japanese military moved. As the Japanese military continued to expand its control, it saw one major obstacle to domination of the Asia-Pacific region—the United States.

On December 7, 1941, Japan conducted a sneak attack on the U.S. military base at Pearl Harbor on Hawaii's island of Oahu. The Japanese military hoped this preemptive strike would destroy the U.S. Pacific forces and enable Japan to move forward, unimpeded, toward building its Asian empire. Following Pearl Harbor, Japan was able to conquer many new lands throughout the South Pacific. Like falling dominoes, the Philippines, Indonesia, Malaya, Burma, Indo-China, and Singapore all fell to Japanese control. It appeared that Japan would soon control all of the South Pacific. The rapid Japanese expansion seemed to pose a potential threat even to India and Australia!

To counter the devastating effect of Pearl Harbor, the

On December 7, 1941, U.S. battleships were hit from the air during the Japanese attack on Pearl Harbor on Hawaii's island of Oahu. Japan's bombing of these U.S. military bases brought the United States into World War II.

United States worked quickly to rebuild its Pacific forces. In June 1942, the United States won a key naval fight in the Battle of Midway. This proved to be a turning point of World War II in the Pacific. After the Battle of Midway, the United States and other allies slowly and systematically chased Japan back to their home islands. The Allies considered the costs of an invasion of Japan. Military experts estimated that hundreds of thousands of American and other Allied soldiers would die. American President Harry S. Truman decided to use a powerful new weapon—the atomic bomb—to convince Japan to surrender.

On August 6, 1945, the United States dropped the first atomic bomb on the city of Hiroshima, killing nearly 100,000 people. Still, Japan showed no sign of surrendering. On August 9, the United States dropped an atomic bomb on Nagasaki, killing nearly 75,000 more people. Japan's military government still would not surrender. With millions of people already dead and millions of others suffering horribly, Emperor Hirohito stepped in. He surrendered, thus ending Japan's tragic World War II saga. The quest for an empire had failed horribly. Japan was devastated and the United States was now stepping in to occupy and rule the nation. The country's humiliation was great. This humiliation, however, was nothing compared with the starvation and suffering of the ordinary Japanese people.

JAPAN AFTER WORLD WAR II

The end of World War II left Japan a badly damaged country. Its industries lay in ruin. Its relationships with virtually all its neighbors were in tatters because of the brutality of its invading armies. In addition, the country was occupied by American forces under General Douglas MacArthur. The Americans drafted a new constitution for Japan, which the Japanese adopted in 1947. The new constitution renounced war forever as a means of settling disputes with other countries. It kept the emperor, but stripped him of most powers. The new government was shaped much like that of the United States. It had a legislature, called the Diet, that was composed of two chambers. It also gave new rights to women. During the first elections, about 35 women were elected to office. Occupation by the United States and the Allies lasted until 1952.

Japanese soldiers turned over their swords to U.S. troops after World War II ended with Japan's unconditional surrender.

The Korean War began in 1950. This nearby conflict gave a great boost to the new industries being built in Japan. In 1951, in San Francisco, Japan agreed to and signed the peace treaty with all of the allies. This treaty formally ended World War II. With this agreement, Japan regained its independence. The country also entered into a mutual defense agreement with the United States.

On its own again by the early 1950s, Japan began an era of remarkable economic growth. Still faced with having few natural resources, the country began to trade with various countries that supplied the needed resources. Industrial production grew at unprecedented rates. Prices of Japanese products were low because of the meager wages paid to workers. This meant that the goods sold well in the international markets. During the two decades following the war, the phrase "Made in Japan" took on the meaning of "cheap products of poor quality." By the late 1960s, however, the meaning began to change. The quality of Japanese products improved, markets expanded, and prosperity returned to the country and its citizens. Names like Toyota, Nissan, Honda, Kawasaki, Sony, Panasonic, and countless others began to symbolize high quality. Japanese products continue to enjoy a reputation for high quality and reasonable prices in today's global marketplace.

Its post-war success led Japan to great gains in the international community. Japan is now a respected member of the United Nations. The country's economic success has been copied by other countries around the world. A very close relationship between business, banking, and government benefited Japan greatly until 1989, when a stock market fall threatened the economy. Today, the closeness of the business, banking, and government sectors seems to work against the country's economy. However, the quality of life enjoyed by Japan's people remains high.

Japan's rise and fall after the Meiji Restoration shows clearly the paths that this small country has used in its attempt to become a world power. The early path of military aggression left the country defeated and humiliated. The peaceful path followed during the second half of the 20th century, however, has made Japan a modern industrial nation with one of the world's highest standards of living. Problems are still evident in the economy, but any visitor to Japan will be impressed with the progress that has been made and the society that exists. No longer a hermit, Japan is now a dynamic country woven into the global fabric with thousands of political, economic, and social threads connecting it to the world.

The love of order and beauty are characteristics of Japanese culture that are expressed through creations such as the traditional Japanese garden.

5

People and Culture

Japan's people and culture are yet another reason the country is often referred to as the "Miracle of the Orient." Japan has successfully blended its traditional East Asian culture with a modern Western urban-industrial way of life. This mixture of the old and the new defines modern Japan.

POPULATION

Japan has an estimated population of 127 million. At first, that figure may not seem very large. In terms of numbers alone, nine countries have more people. But such facts and figures fail to tell the whole story.

In total area, Japan is slightly smaller than California, which, with about 34 million people, is the most populated state in the United States. But Japan's population is nearly four times greater than that of California! In fact, Japan's population is nearly half that of the entire United States. Like California, however, much of Japan is sparsely settled. Because so much of Japan is mountainous, the population is concentrated in just a few cities and towns. This means the places that people actually live in Japan are densely populated, with thousands of people per square mile (square kilometer). In fact, few places in the world are as crowded as Japanese cities.

POPULATION CHARACTERISTICS

Demographic data show that Japan's population is unique in many respects. In a land with few resources, little agricultural land, and many environmental hazards, several aspects of the country's demography are, indeed, miracles—not only for Asia, but for the world.

Japan long ago came to grips with its population "explosion." Today, with an annual growth rate estimated to be 0.15 percent, the country is approaching zero population growth. In fact, the Japanese government believes that the rate of population increase is too low. Current projections suggest that by the year 2050, the country's population actually will decline by an estimated 21 percent. This is why, despite the country's having such a high population density, the government is encouraging families to have more children.

With so few births, another problem Japan faces is an aging population. The average Japanese person can expect to live about 81 years. No other country can match this longevity. As is true in the United States, most Japanese retire in their 60s. This means that a growing number of people are living well beyond the age of employment. With fewer young people in the work force, providing for the elderly has become an increasing challenge for society.

The Japanese people enjoy a high standard of living. Income, of course, is one important factor. Among major world nations, Japan's per capita income and gross national product ranks near the top. Income alone, however, does not always mean a high standard of living. In some countries, only the wealthy few benefit. In Japan, wealth is fairly evenly distributed among the population. This has an important influence on the population. If people are able to afford health care, for example, the results will be reflected in life expectancy. Japan's high standard of living influences other demographic data, too. At 3.7 deaths per 1,000 births, Japan has one of the world's lowest infant mortality rates. (Infant mortality rates in the United States, by comparison, are about 6.7 deaths per 1,000 births.) Japan also has one of the world's highest literacy rates—about 99 percent of people over the age of 15 can read and write.

OVERPOPULATED?

Overpopulation is a difficult concept to define. Some people examine population numbers and population density when defining the concept. Others look at such factors as per capita income, gross domestic product, life expectancy, literacy, and other signs to judge whether a country suffers from overpopulation. Numbers of people seem to be of minor importance. After all, some of the world's most populated places also have the world's highest standards of living. On the other hand, some countries have a very low population density, yet their people live short and miserable lives.

Japan, despite its large population and high population density, also enjoys a high standard of living. In fact, the Japanese people are the country's most important resource. Human resources, rather than a large area and an abundance of natural resources, have made it possible for Japan to prosper. There are many definitions of "overpopulation." Considering the good health of the Japanese people and economy, it is doubtful that any definition of overpopulation applies to Japan.

SETTLEMENT

Flying into or out of Tokyo's Narita International Airport on a clear night is an amazing experience. The Tokyo-Yokohama metropolitan area is among the world's most densely populated places. Here, nearly 30 million people are squeezed into an area of only about 1,700 square miles (4,400 square kilometers)—an area just slightly larger than Los Angeles County, but with more than twice as many people!

Flying southward, having left the huge urban complex, the land below and to the west is mountainous. Only a few small dots of light appear. To the east, along the coastal plain, the string of light from cities and towns is nearly unbroken. Soon airplane passengers can see a huge island of light from the combined cities of Osaka and Kobe. Here, another 14 to 15 million people are packed into an area of only 880 square miles (2,280 square kilometers).

The short flight between these two huge cities serves as a wonderful introduction to two primary characteristics of Japan's settlement patterns. First, it is a country of large cities, 10 of which have populations of more than 1 million. In fact, 78 percent of all Japanese live in cities or large towns. This figure is all the more remarkable, however, when one realizes that about 80 percent of the country is mountainous. In the rugged highland areas, there are few towns or people. At night, much of Japan appears to be dark from the air. But the islands of light created by Tokyo-Yokohama, Osaka-Kobe, Nagoya, Kyoto, and other huge Japanese cities clearly demonstrate the country's pattern of urban settlement.

A HOMOGENEOUS PEOPLE

Japan has one of the world's most homogeneous populations. Over 98 percent of the country's inhabitants are ethnic Japanese. This means that most Japanese share similar physical features, such as black hair. They also share a way of life, including cultural roots, traditions, and practices.

Tokyo, Japan's capital, is one of the most densely populated cities in the world.

In Japan, *gaijin* (outsiders) truly do stand out. The country does have a few "minority" people. Koreans make up the largest group of foreign people, with about 500,000 living in Japan. There also are small numbers of Chinese, Brazilians, Filipinos, and Americans living in the country. In the United States, diversity is taken for granted, particularly in cities. Food, for example, is a wonderful indicator of diverse tastes. In any large American city one can select from Italian, Chinese, Mexican, Greek, German, Thai, and perhaps several dozen other types of cuisine—including Japanese. Throughout Japan, however, food, dress, appearance, customs, language, religion, and all other aspects of culture are quite similar.

JAPANESE CULTURE

Cultures are complex. They include every aspect of peoples' way of life. This includes how people think, act, and relate to one another. It also includes how they live, where, and in what kinds of settlements and dwellings. And how they communicate, worship, make a living, and govern themselves. The remainder of this chapter focuses on what are two of the most important aspects of any culture—language and religion.

LANGUAGE

Japanese is the official language of the country. Spoken Japanese is different than other Asian languages, such as Chinese or Korean. Its rules of grammar and pronunciation are quite simple, making spoken Japanese a relatively easy language to learn. Many scholars who study languages, however, believe that the written form of Japanese may be the world's most complex and difficult to learn. Three types of characters are used in Japanese writing: *kanji, hiragana,* and *katakana.* Kanji reached Japan from China, by way of the Korean Peninsula, in ancient times. Each kanji character (there are at least 48,000) is an ideogram, or a picture that represents a thing or an idea. Some characters require as many as 23 separate strokes to write.

Japanese was a spoken language long before it was written. The kanji alphabet was unable to express many of the sounds of Japanese words. In order to overcome this problem, the Japanese developed two other sets of characters. These writing systems, hiragana and katakana, were developed from the original *kanji* characters. Each is similar to letters in the English alphabet, because each character represents a single phonetic sound. Hiragana and Katakana are much easier to write than kanji, because characters are written with no more than four strokes.

Traditional Japanese handwriting is very artistic. But it can be extremely confusing to people who are not native speakers. In modern written Japanese, for example, kanji, hiragana, and katakana are combined. Kanji characters are used for the main body of a written work. Hiragana characters are used in writing verb endings, adverbs, and short linking words. Most foreign terms are written in the more flexible katakana style. In addition to the three sets of characters used, Japanese writing differs greatly from other forms in yet another way. Traditionally, at least, Japanese is written vertically and read from right to left and top to bottom of the page.

Today, most Japanese are able to speak and write at least some English. Students learn the English language in secondary school. Increasingly, it is the language of global business, tourism, media, entertainment, and computer applications.

RELIGION

Freedom of religion is guaranteed by the Japanese consti-tution. Religious beliefs and practices in Japan revolve around two faiths—Shintoism and Buddhism. Shinto, meaning "the way of the gods," is an ancient faith that is native to Japan. It is a philosophy that is concerned primarily with the living (present) world. Shinto also involves ancestor worship. Buddhism originated in India and reached Japan in the 6th century A.D. from Korea. It is a faith the focuses on enlighten-ment and meditation. Shinto gates (called *torii*) and other shrines and Buddhist statues are common features of the Japanese landscape.

Major life events, such as weddings, are normally held in Shinto shrines. Buddhist priests usually perform the funerals. To many Americans, religious practices in Japan may appear to be strange. For example, when surveyed about their religious beliefs, most Japanese are vague. Rarely do they boldly and proudly claim affiliation with any particular faith. Another striking trait of the Japanese people is that a sub-stantial number of them, an estimated 85 percent, follow practices of both Shintoism and Buddhism. In order to under-stand how such a dual belief system can exist, one must recognize the different roles that the respective religions fulfill. "Shintoism," one Japanese person explained, "is for now [the living world], and Buddhism is for later [after death]."

The temple of the Golden Pavilion in Kyoto is one of the many
extraordinary sites in Japan. Originally built in the late 14th century,
the temple is covered by 100,000 sheets of gold paper.

Because of the different functions each religion performs,
more than half of all Japanese homes have both a small
Buddhist altar and Shinto shrine.

Another difference between most Japanese people and
Christians or Jews is that most Japanese do not believe in just
one god. Rather, their worldview includes many *kami*, Shinto
gods or spirits with varying degrees of power. Finally, Japanese
society is much more secular than the United States. That is,

religion does not play as important a role in the life of most people as it does for many Americans.

The Japanese worldview is much different than that of Christians. In the Christian view, religion often defines one's identity. Japanese, on the other hand, tend to be much more open-minded and practical in their worldview. They do not hesitate to turn to science for answers, yet many will also turn to one or more alternative sources of aid. When a Japanese person becomes ill, for example, he or she almost certainly will seek the aid of a trained physician. Meanwhile, the person also may turn to a person trained in herbal folk medicine or visit a Shinto shrine. The physician attempts to cure the patient using modern medicine. The herbalist believes the body is out of balance, a situation that can be cured with the appropriate use of certain herbs. Visiting a shrine, many Japanese people believe, purifies the mind, which is necessary if the body is to heal.

Japan has a democratic form of government where citizens elect government leaders to represent them. In 2001, Japanese Prime Minister Junichiro Koizumi (center) celebrated his political party's landslide victory in elections.

6

Government

Japan adopted its current constitution in 1947. The Japanese constitution established the country as a constitutional monarchy. This means that Japan is a democracy where the people rule indirectly through their representatives in the Diet, the Japanese Parliament. The constitution gives all citizens 20 years of age and older the right to vote. Under the constitution, the emperor has almost no power. Instead, he serves as a symbol of the country. The emperor, however, does appoint key public officials like the prime minister and chief justice. This is only a formality, however, and not a political requirement. This situation is much like the role of the royal family in the United Kingdom. An important national holiday in Japan is the emperor's birthday.

BRANCHES OF GOVERNMENT

Japan has three branches of government: the legislative branch, the executive branch, and the judicial branch. Japan's legislative branch of government is called the Diet. The Diet has the power to make laws in Japan. This body has two chambers: the House of Representatives and the House of Councillors. Each of these houses is independent of the other and the members of each are elected directly by the citizens.

The House of Councillors, or *Sangi-in*, has 252 members. Of these, 100 are elected by the nation as a whole and 152 are elected by voters in smaller districts. The members of the House of Councillors must be at least 30 years old. They serve 6-year terms.

The House of Representatives, or *Shugi-in*, is larger than the House of Councillors. There are 480 members in the House of Representatives and they serve 4-year terms unless the government is dissolved earlier. If dissolved, there must be new elections for the House of Representatives within 40 days. In elections, 300 of the members are elected from single-member districts and the other 180 are elected from 11 regions around the country who gain their seats based on a proportional basis of the votes cast. Members of the House of Representatives must be at least 25 years old.

Bills become laws after they are passed by both houses of the Diet. The House of Representatives controls the national budget and approves treaties. Most other matters can be raised in either of the two houses.

The executive branch of the government is headed by the prime minister. The prime minister is responsible for administering the laws of Japan and for managing foreign affairs, making treaties, and preparing the budget that the Diet reviews. One of the major responsibilities of the Diet is to elect the prime minister. The prime minister must be a member of the Diet. In fact, the leader of the majority party in the Diet is usually the person who serves as prime minister. Prime ministers have no limits placed on the length of time they can serve in office. One

Emperor Akihito (left) is the head of the Japanese government. His power, however, is largely ceremonial.

served for almost 12 years. However, the prime minister can be removed with a no-confidence vote in the Diet. This can greatly shorten a prime minister's term. One only held office for 54 days!

Since World War II, most of the prime ministers have come from the Liberal Democratic Party (LDP). This party has held power since 1955 with the exception of a 3-year stretch in the mid-1990s. During this time the LDP was removed from office because of a major corruption scandal that tainted the government and the party.

The prime minister selects members of the Cabinet to help govern the country. Under the constitution, a majority of Cabinet members must be members of the Diet. Cabinet members also must be civilians. This is to prevent the military from gaining too much power as it did before World War II.

The judicial branch of government is responsible for interpreting the laws of the country. The Supreme Court is the highest court in Japan. This court is headed by a chief justice and several lesser justices. Today, there are 15 members serving on the court. The chief justice of the Supreme Court is recommended by the Cabinet and appointed by the emperor. The emperor's appointment is only a formality; the emperor does not have real political power. All other Supreme Court judges are appointed directly by the Cabinet.

The Supreme Court is the court of last resort. This means that its decisions are final and there are no other appeals that can be made. Therefore, it is empowered to rule on the constitutionality of any laws, orders, or actions.

Other types of courts fall below the Supreme Court. These include the high courts that are directly under the Supreme Court. Under the high courts are the family courts and district courts. The lowest court level is the summary court. Cases from any of the lower courts can be appealed to a higher court by the side that is dissatisfied with the lower court's decision.

Japan's constitution provides the groundwork for local government in the country. Japan is divided into 47 districts, called prefectures. Beneath these are over 3,000 local governments at the town, village, and city level. Like most local governments in the world, Japan's local governments deal with important issues that lie close to home, such as garbage collection, healthcare, and schools.

FOREIGN AFFAIRS

Japan's constitution provides an element that is not found in other such documents. The constitution states that "the Japanese people forever renounce war as a right of the sovereign nation." Because of the horror of World War II and the damage caused by nuclear bombs at Hiroshima and Nagasaki, Japan renounced war forever.

The constitution further provides that Japan shall maintain no land, sea, or air forces. This section of the constitution is often challenged when Japan faces threats by other forces. For example, the Japanese became upset when North Korea test fired a missile that traveled directly over the islands of Japan. China and Japan also have a tenuous history that could promote Japan remilitarizing. Presently Japan depends on the United States to defend its security as pledged in the United States-Japan Security Treaty of 1951. Even with this agreement, many Japanese are uncertain whether the United States would actually step in and defend Japan. Whether Japan changes its constitution and removes the Renunciation of War section will be an issue that will be followed with interest by the rest of the world.

Japan was isolated during much of its history. This is no longer the case. Today Japan is widely engaged in activities around the planet. It is a major economic power and political power with influence regionally and globally. Japan is now a major trading power with most other nations in the world. Its major trading partners are the United States, China, European Union, Australia, South Korea, and nations in Southeast Asia. Politically, Japan is a member of many international organizations and has signed many significant international agreements. Simply put, Japan is a major player in the world today.

Japan has been an active member of the United Nations since 1956. It has served on the important Security Council and has contributed to various United Nations collective security actions, such as mine sweeping in the Persian Gulf and sending peacekeeping forces to Cambodia. Its role in promoting peace and international security has increased in recent years.

An example of Japan's new leadership is found in its hosting of the Kyoto Protocol in December of 1997. Nations from around the world came together to meet in the Japanese city of Kyoto to discuss the problem of global warming. They signed an agreement called the Kyoto Protocol, which establishes a formula for how much gaseous pollution developed countries can emit into the atmosphere.

Since World War II, Japan has again become a leader among countries. Its economy and foreign policy link it to other countries around the world. The country was on a political and economic roller coaster ride during the 20th century with many frightening ups and downs. Now it is a democratic society that has regained the respect of the world.

At the port city of Chiba in January 2003, about 3,000 Honda cars wait to be shipped to North America. Japan's strong economy is built on exports.

7

The Economy

When people call Japan the "Miracle of the Orient," they are usually referring to the country's economy. In this chapter, you will learn how the Japanese had to overcome many obstacles in order to become one of the world's foremost economic powers. You also will learn why the country's economy has been in a decade-long slump and why many Japanese are concerned about their country's economic future.

JAPAN AND THE GLOBAL ECONOMY

To better understand Japan's position among the world's economic giants, think for a moment about your own family possessions. Perhaps you own a vehicle, television, camera, or other item made by a Japanese company. A typical American family has many thousands of dollars worth of items manufactured by Japanese corporations.

Now, try to identify those "big ticket" items that were manufactured in Europe. If you can only find a few items, or perhaps
none, you are not alone. You also have just learned a very
important lesson in changing patterns of global economic and
regional geography!

Nearly a quarter of a century ago, the center of world trade
shifted from the North Atlantic Ocean (North America and
Europe) to the Pacific Rim. Today, about three-fourths of all
world trade is conducted among Pacific Rim countries. The
primary "engines" of this multi-trillion dollar trade, of course,
are the United States and Japan. In fact, according to 2002
World Bank data, the combined economies of the United States
and Japan amounted to a staggering $14.42 trillion. To put
this figure in perspective, it is roughly equal to that of the
next 35 countries, those ranking number 3 through number
37, combined!

HOW WELL OFF ARE THE JAPANESE?

There are many ways to measure a country's economic
health. One way is to look at its gross domestic product (GDP).
The GDP is the total value of all goods and services produced
in a country per year. Japan ranks second among the world's
nations in its GDP. This tells only part of the country's economic
story, however. For example, when Japan's GDP is divided by its
127 million people, the country drops to 14th place among
world nations in terms of per capita (per person) GDP. This
means that people in at least 13 other countries produce more
wealth per person.

In terms of purchasing power, the Japanese rank 13th in the
world, and are not as well off as Americans. Because prices of
most items are much higher in Japan than in the United States,
it costs more to live there. To help rank countries by buying
power, economists have developed the concept of purchasing
power parity (PPP). A country's PPP indicates how much buying power its people have. In 2002, the United States ranked

number 3 in the world, with a per capita PPP of $34,870. Japan ranked 13th in the world, with a per capita PPP of $27,430. In other words, the average American can buy nearly $35,000 worth of goods in a year, while the average Japanese can purchase just over $27,000 worth of goods in a year.

By any measure, however, most Japanese are quite comfortable economically. Few countries enjoy a better distribution of income. Most Japanese belong to the economic middle class and few citizens suffer from grinding poverty. The Japanese also save a greater percentage of their income than do almost any other people. In fact, several years ago it was estimated that the typical Japanese family had $40,000 in savings, whereas the average American family was $40,000 in debt!

Until the economic downturn that began in the early 1990s, few Japanese were unemployed. Today, for the first time in many years, unemployment is rising. In early 2003, an estimated 5.5 percent of the Japanese work force was without jobs. This number represents an all-time high figure and is a source of great pain, embarrassment, and concern to the country. This figure is quite low, however, when compared to that of many other countries. To the Japanese, a loss of a job can result in a loss of pride. A number of unemployed people are ashamed to face their family and friends. Moreover, suicides have risen at an alarming rate—to one of the world's highest. Faced with possible loss of employment, the Japanese have developed perhaps the world's best work ethic. In fact, they have a word with no equivalent in the English language: *karoshi*. This is a Japanese term for "death from overwork," a condition in which Japan may be the world leader.

OVERCOMING OBSTACLES

Few countries have faced a greater number of obstacles to economic growth than has Japan. Certainly very few nations have been more successful than Japan in overcoming such hurdles. In this respect, Japan truly is the "Miracle of the Orient."

Much of Japanese rice farming is still done by hand. Japanese farms, although small, produce some of the world's highest crop yields.

Japan is confronted by several major physical obstacles to economic growth and development. These obstacles include small area, fragmentation and elongation, devastating environmental hazards, remote and insular location, and limited natural resources.

Most of Japan is composed of rugged, mountainous land. In fact, only about 30,000 square miles (77,700 square kilometers) is relatively flat land suited to farming and urban development. This is an area roughly the size of South Carolina, a state which is home to fewer than 4 million people. Japan, with a population of some 127 million, packs roughly 35 times more people into a comparable area.

Small size, however, has not proved to be a significant handicap. Few of the world's people use land more effectively than do the Japanese. Much of the country is built at what appears to be a "micro scale." The Japanese are extremely efficient in the use of land, whether in farming, urban development,

Tuna meat is inspected at the Tsukji Fish Market in Tokyo. Throughout most of the 20th century, Japan was the world leader in fishing, including the size of its fishing fleet and the amount of its catch.

transportation, or other aspects of living and producing. Agriculture is extremely productive, much of it relying on intensive hand labor. Japanese farms produce the world's highest yields of many crops.

The Japanese diet depends heavily upon marine resources. Throughout most of the 20th century, Japan was the world leader in fishing. The country also is a major importer of seafood. Japan does not need to raise a large percentage of its own food. The country's strong economy enables it to import food and other commodities from countries throughout the world. The United States, in fact, is Japan's leading source of imported foodstuffs.

As you know, Japan is composed of four major islands and more than 3,000 smaller islands and islets. Additionally, these islands are scattered over a huge area measuring roughly 3,000 miles (4,800 kilometers) along a relatively narrow northeasterly to southwesterly axis. Geographers realize that fragmentation and elongation often lead to internal isolation. This, in turn, often contributes to a number of forces that tend to tear a country apart, such as regional conflicts. To the south, the island country of Indonesia offers an example of this situation. The country has nearly 600 different languages, a weak government, and suffers from a long history of internal conflicts.

In spite of its scattered physical geography, Japan is one of the world's most cohesive countries. The Japanese share a strong common heritage and sense of nationalism. Few countries in the world can match Japan's strong social, cultural, and racial cohesion, or sense of national unity. This means that nearly all Japanese people are willing to work and sacrifice for their country and for the well-being of their fellow countrymen.

Japan has overcome fragmentation by developing one of the world's best transportation networks. Railroad, air, water, and automobile facilities provide quick and easy access to nearly the entire country. People, materials, ideas, foodstuffs, and other items can be quickly and efficiently moved from place to place.

Japan faces several environmental dangers, including earthquakes, volcanoes, and landslides. Yet, the Japanese have been able to minimize the impact of nature's wrath in a number of ways. They lead the world in emergency training and warning systems. When disaster strikes, the Japanese know how to respond. Nearly all Japanese construction is designed to withstand most earthquakes. Japanese engineers are world leaders in developing means of protecting the country's coastal regions from storm and tsunami damage. Finally, smart planning and zoning limit the development of sites that are hazard prone. Because of these measures, when disaster does strike, damage often is minimal. When the 1995 earthquake hit Kobe and nearby cities, Japan's strong economy and government assistance enabled people to recovery quickly.

Great distance to global ideas and markets has posed few problems for the Japanese. Japan has overcome its remote location in a number of ways. In terms of the flow of ideas and information, during the last half of the 20th century, Japan became a world leader in communications technology. To overcome great distances by sea, the country became the world's leading shipbuilder and ship owner. To reduce transportation costs, Japanese industry has specialized in high value/low bulk manufactured goods. Cameras, watches, small tools, and other high value manufactured goods weigh very little, hence, cost little to ship—regardless of the distance. Because it is an island nation, all but the smallest and most valuable goods are transported by ship. This is the least expensive means of transportation. The per unit cost of shipping a new car from Japan to the western coast of the United States, for example, is less than trucking the vehicle from Los Angeles to a dealership in Phoenix, Arizona.

Japan has almost no natural resources upon which to base industrial development. In the West, the Industrial Revolution was fueled by huge deposits of inexpensive and readily available coal. Abundant and inexpensive energy is often the key to a country's economic growth. Metals and other minerals also can be extremely important. Yet, Japan must import fully 97 percent of the natural resources and raw materials used in its industry. The only resource the country has in abundance is hydroelectric potential, which for all practical purposes is 100 percent developed.

Geographers, economists, and other social scientists have long recognized that well-educated, hard-working people—rather than abundant natural resources—are the key to economic development. The Japanese are highly disciplined, ambitious, and work extremely well as teams. They have perhaps the world's strongest work ethic. One survey found that more than 90 percent of all Japanese adults preferred work to leisure, and the government had to pass a law requiring Japanese workers to take their annual vacation! They also are very well educated and highly skilled. Their sales force may be the world's best trained and most successful.

Japan's huge success in competing in the global marketplace can be attributed to a simple "P-Q-R-S-T" formula: "P" stands for productivity and pride. Japanese workers strive for a high level of productivity and take great pride in what they produce. "Q" means quality. Japanese products are world famous for their quality of design and manufacture. "R" indicates robotization. The Japanese are world leaders in using robots, rather than humans, to do many industrial tasks. This frees people to do more important things that better use their knowledge, energy, and skills. "S" refers to sales and savings, two categories in which the Japanese are world leaders. To the American salesperson, "time is money." The Japanese use a completely different approach. They seek to gain the confidence, friendship, and loyalty of a potential buyer before attempting to make a sale. Relative to people in most other countries, the Japanese save large amounts of their income. This provides capital that can be recirculated into the nation's economy (as bank loans, for example). Finally, "T" stands for technology, an area in which the Japanese have become world leaders on par with the United States. In fact, Japan and the United States often vie for the top position in the number of new patents issued annually.

CULTURAL AND HISTORICAL OBSTACLES

On the road to becoming a leading economic power, Japan also had several cultural and historical obstacles to surmount. They include a long period of cultural isolation, a late start in the Industrial Revolution, and the devastating effects of World War II.

For 300 years prior to the mid-19th century, Japan deliberately isolated itself from the rest of the world. The door to Japan was cracked open slightly by Commodore Perry in 1853. By 1868, the Meiji Restoration threw the door open wide and what came to be known as Japan's "economic miracle" began. During the Meiji period, several important developments set the stage for Japan's future in the world. Japan's rulers place great emphasis on education. Literacy among Japanese people soared. It was a period of relative political stability and the government enthusiastically supported economic development. Western technology was readily adopted and quickly adapted to Japan's culture and society. Finally, as a unified people, the Japanese worked together for the good of their country.

By the 1860s, Japan was lagging a century or more behind the already industrialized West. It had a long way to go if it was to catch up. During the Meiji Restoration, the Japanese eagerly adopted a number of Western ideas and techniques associated with the Industrial Revolution. So successful was this transformation that by 1935, manufacturing surpassed agriculture as the most important contributor to Japan's economy. Industrial growth also allowed Japan to aggressively challenge the world's greatest military powers.

Japan became involved in World War II for two primary reasons. First, it sought to gain control of vital natural resources and additional territory on the Asian mainland. Second, it attempted to create a "buffer" in the Pacific Basin as protection from the United States. The ultimate result of this venture was near total devastation.

Once again, the Japanese successfully overcame what seemed to be an almost insurmountable obstacle. After the war, the United States invested millions of dollars in rebuilding Japan. From the ashes of war rose hundreds of new factories using the most modern technology available. The Americans helped the Japanese draft a new constitution that contributed to a more democratic government and society. The document also limited Japan's military expenditures to 1 percent of the country's annual gross national product. With virtually no military expenses, the Japanese could pour huge amounts of capital into industrial growth and development. Japanese scientists and inventors also were able to emphasize commercial, rather than military, innovations. Within several decades, Japan once again held a high place among the world's economic powers.

TROUBLED TIMES

Since the early 1990s, Japan's economy has weakened. By some measures, it has even slipped from second to third place among the world's economic giants, behind the United States and China. The country has undergone the worst economic slump since the Great Depression ravaged the global economy in the 1930s. Its stock market has lost nearly 80 percent of its value since 1990. Real estate values have plummeted and countless banks and businesses have failed. Its national debt is four times greater than that of the United States. The value of production and services is dropping and retail sales have plunged as Japanese have tightened their spending habits. Guaranteed lifetime employment, enjoyed by many Japanese for decades, is disappearing and unemployment has risen to record levels. These surely are troubled times for the country's economy and its people.

What went wrong? During the 1980s, many observers predicted that Japan would soon surpass the United States as the world's strongest economy. Several factors contributed to Japan's weakening economy. First, as the world's leading exporter of manufactured goods, Japan is extremely vulnerable to changes in the global economy. During the past decade, the United States and most other industrial economies have undergone economic hard times. When this occurs, people are less apt to buy high-quality, relatively expensive, Japanese goods.

Many people point to the Japanese government as another significant problem. Political corruption is widespread in Japan, and many people have lost faith in their government.

Japanese leaders have failed to pass much needed political reforms (such as within the banking industry, which is on the brink of collapse because of trillions of dollars in bad loans). According to many social scientists, no end is in sight for Japan's economic woes. The problems are many and the solutions are both complex and painful.

Is Japan finished as a leading economic power? The answer, almost certainly, is no. The country has surmounted many obstacles to reach its current level of economic strength. Today, the Japanese are still well-to-do by most standards, including those of the United States. According to surveys, nearly two-thirds of the country's people remain satisfied with their lives. And satisfied, well-educated, hard-working people, we must remember, remain Japan's primary resource and hope for continued economic success.

A Japanese family prepares to eat dinner. They are kneeling on *tatami* mats, which are found in many Japanese homes.

Living in Japan Today

O ne of the Japanese peoples' greatest strengths is the ability to adopt ideas and values from other cultures, and then adapt them to their own lives. This marvelous ability is evident in their religion, writing systems, housing, and even food. Yet the Japanese also preserve their own values and beliefs. In this chapter, we will look at lifestyles of the people of Japan, keeping in mind that living in Japan today also means honoring the past.

FOOD

With no place in Japan being more than about 100 miles from the sea, a diet of seafood nourishes the population. Warm *kuroshio* currents meet with the cold *oyashio* currents to provide some of the world's richest fishing grounds. Eating beef and pork was forbidden at the end of the 17th century when Buddhist teachings were enforced. This belief, combined with a lack of grazing land for farm animals, further established the habits of a fish-eating country. Health benefits of a low-fat diet composed of fish and rice, two staples of Japanese meals, have nurtured long life expectancies for the Japanese population.

Fish is a main element in the Japanese diet and is eaten in a variety of ways—steamed, fried, boiled, broiled, and raw. Raw fish is considered a delicacy in Japan. Raw fish may be served as *sushi,* in thin slices on top of small mounds of rice that have been cooked with vinegar, rice wine, and sugar. Many visitors who try raw fish for the first time are pleasantly surprised by its delicate flavor and aroma. Another food resource from the sea is *nori,* a type of dark green seaweed that is pressed into flat sheets and dried. Cut into small rectangles, *nori* is eaten by wrapping it around rice, often with other seafood or vegetables.

Rice, the main staple of the Japanese diet, is eaten with most meals regardless of the time of day. In fact, if you are not at home to prepare the rice, it is available in cooked form from vending machines! These ever-present machines are available throughout Japan and not only offer cooked rice for purchase, but also books, hot and cold drinks, compact discs, and even mobile phones!

Language of a culture often provides clues to values and concepts within that culture. For example, in Japan the importance of rice in the daily diet is revealed in the word *gohan,* which means both "cooked rice" and "meal." This word is extended to *asagohan* (breakfast), *hirugohan* (lunch), and *bangohan* (dinner). These words indicate the powerful association of rice in all Japanese meals.

When traveling in Japan, tempting displays of food entice hungry customers. Realistic and appealing in appearance, plastic food models are often displayed in restaurant windows to tempt potential customers. Another delightful meal option is the *obento,* a box lunch consisting of rice, vegetables, fish, and often a dessert such as a red bean cake. *Obento* are sold at many train stations, department stores, and convenience stores.

In recent years, the Japanese have been eating less rice and more poultry and meat. Chicken and pork are relatively inexpensive and fairly plentiful. Beef, however, is quite expensive and not as plentiful. Skillet dishes, such as *sukiyaki* (a dish of sliced meat and vegetables cooked in sweetened soy sauce), are commonly served in Japan. *Tempura* is another popular dish. This is a combination of various vegetables and fish deep-fried in a light batter. *Udon*, noodles made of wheat flour, are served in a broth with vegetables.

To eat these foods, the Japanese use *hashi* (chopsticks). By the age of three, many children have mastered the use of *hashi* after using trainer *hashi* with special handles for their fingers. Knives, spoons, and forks are also used by all generations when eating western-style foods. Hamburgers, pizza, Chinese food, curry, and spaghetti are all available in Japan. In urban areas, one is never far from fast-food restaurants, including McDonald's and Kentucky Fried Chicken.

Since World War II, the Japanese diet has changed to include fast food and other westernized food options. As a result, Japanese people are growing taller and heavier. The average height for 14-year-old Japanese males has increased by more than 7 inches since 1945. The average weight for Japanese males of this age has increased by more than 30 pounds.

HOUSING

Houses in Japan are designed for maximum ventilation. Most interior rooms have one or two walls that consist of sliding doors called *fusuma*. These doors can be opened or closed, along with sliding doors on outside walls, to provide a fresh breeze or to prevent drafts.

When entering a Japanese home, one first steps into the *genkan*. This small, wooden-floored area is where you remove

Many houses in Japan are designed with doors that can be opened or closed to provide a fresh breeze or to prevent drafts. These sliding doors, which in fact are sliding walls, are called *fusuma*.

your shoes, placing them neatly side by side facing the door through which you just entered. The *genkan* is not just a physical space, it also serves an important and symbolic cultural function. While you are physically inside the house, this transition area provides guests and family members a space to enter politely, with culturally appropriate behavior, into the home. Slippers are then put on and worn throughout the house as you take one step up (again a physical and cultural function) to enter the main level of the home.

Japanese homes have a separate room for bathing, away

from the toilet room. In Japan, you clean your body *before* getting into the bathtub! A small plastic stool rests next to a drain in the tiled floor. Here, one sits to wash with soap and rinse off before entering the full bathtub of heated water. Once clean, you then enter the soaking luxury of a small, deep bathtub filled with heated water reaching up to your neck. Since each person enters the bathtub clean, the entire family can use the same tub of hot water.

Winter is generally mild in much of Japan, with the exception of the much colder winters of Hokkaido in the north. Most houses typically have no centralized heating. Rather, rooms used for daily living are located in the center of the house and heated by small heaters. Often in winter, members of a family sit around a *kotatsu*, a low table with an electric heater beneath it. A quilt is placed over the *kotatsu* so that you can slip your legs and feet under the blanket while sitting on pillows. What a comforting way to eat, watch television, or share conversation with your family!

Japanese houses are typically smaller than western-style houses. In Tokyo, homes tend to be even smaller due to population densities and scarcity of land. Since Japanese homes are small, rooms serve multiple functions such as living, eating, studying, or sleeping. To utilize space wisely, a *futon* (soft folding mattress) is often spread out on the floor at night for sleeping. After being aired and folded, the *futon* is stored in a closet during the day. Except for the kitchen and perhaps a carpeted living room (a western adaptation), the floors in Japanese homes are covered with joining straw mats called *tatami*. The mats are comfortable to sit on, sleep on (with a futon), and walk on without slippers. *Tatami* also provide a layer of insulation in the cooler winter months.

Many homes are built with mixed styles of traditional *tatami* mat rooms and western-style carpeted rooms. Sleeping on futons or sleeping in beds is another choice being made by members of Japanese families today.

The compact size of a Japanese home is well adapted to the needs of Japanese society. Family members live together closely and must resolve conflicts in behavior. Outside the home, Japanese like to feel that they belong to a group. Importance is placed on harmony and cooperation in human relationships. Much practice at home makes this trait a more natural process in one's way of interacting with others outside of the home.

HOME AND FAMILY

Until recently, many Japanese lived in extended families of three or more generations. Grandparents, and sometimes great-grandparents, were important and respected members of the household. Traditions and family heritage was shared with members of the family. But rapid economic growth and the process of democratization following World War II have influenced the Japanese family. Family life is changing from an extended multigenerational family to that of a nuclear family consisting of parents and children only.

Japanese lifestyle has also been influenced by urbanization and advances in technology. Widespread use of timesaving household appliances, expansion of instant and frozen food industries, and increased popularity and ease of including western-style meals are conveniences enjoyed by many Japanese families. These conveniences have freed more time for both leisure and educational pursuits, especially for women who were often restricted by household tasks.

Increasing employment opportunities for women have changed the Japanese family. Delaying marriage and delaying or choosing not to have children, are changing women's traditional roles in the family. With a present birth rate of .15 percent, the population of Japan will not be able to maintain stability and growth, an alarming concern for the Japanese government and society as a whole. Fewer extended families, combined with increased life expectancies, means the number of elderly people living on their own has also risen significantly. Additional issues of healthcare and housing for the elderly are concerns facing Japanese society today.

A CHANGING SOCIETY

Japan is experiencing a change in the work environment as well. Employees are yearning for more emotional fulfillment from their jobs, calling for reduced working hours and more opportunities for career changes and family time. Once a source of pride and admiration for Japan, the employment market is showing worrisome trends. Rising joblessness among young people (ages 15–24) has resulted from dramatic changes in their behaviors and attitudes toward employment. Soaring numbers of university graduates do not have full-time employment upon graduation and are not as likely to go on to graduate schools. Increasing numbers of young Japanese are also more widely accepting a "*freeter*" lifestyle. (Freeter is a Japanese compound word developed from the English word "free" and the German word "arbeiter" meaning worker.) More and more young people are continuing to live at home, dependent on their parents and working without regular or advancing employment.

This change in attitudes toward work among Japan's young generations has a significant effect. The collapse of the Japanese economy in the early 1990s meant fewer university graduates were hired as full-time workers by Japanese companies. Employers began to hire more part-time workers in order to reduce costs. Traditionally, Japanese companies provided lifetime employment for the *sarariman* (salary man). In return for employment and other benefits, the *sarariman* was expected to devote many hours to his work and company during his lifetime. Companies in the past typically provided their own training for university graduates. Thus, Japanese universities tended to have relative unimportance for preparing graduates with a specific, clear vision of their career goals or providing support for career planning. Today, Japanese companies are seeking to hire students who can make immediate contributions to the company. This means that universities must alter how they train students.

EDUCATION

A young person's educational background is a vital factor in gaining employment. Students who graduate from top universities have an advantage over others when seeking employment. To qualify for admission to top universities, students devote many hours to intense study. Students prepare for entrance exams by attending private academies (called *juku*) after regular school hours. The intensity of *juku* combined with the demands of regular homework leaves students little leisure time. Increases in suicides among youth and a troublesome trend of students showing little interest in studying are perceived as issues of an educational system needing changes. It is the desire of the Japanese to continue serious efforts to make educational opportunities more effective for students.

Japanese students typically attend school for 240 days, approximately 60 days more than students in the United States. The school year begins in April. Japanese schools used to have a 6-day school week, having only Sundays off. In the past decade this changed to 2 or 3 Saturdays per month off. Presently, many schools are now following a 5-day school week at the recommendation of educational advisors. Surprisingly, neither students nor teachers are happy with the new 5-day schedule! The Japanese, it seems, recognize the tremendous importance of education both to individuals and to their country.

Prior to the national education system that was established in Japan more than 100 years ago, various schools served the needs of the differing social classes. Special schools were established for children of the warrior class, for wealthy members of

Students line up in a Tokyo schoolyard and prepare to exercise. Most students in Japan wear school uniforms.

the merchant and farming classes, and for the children of the lower classes.

The national education system developed elementary and secondary schools throughout Japan for all children. Students progress through the stages of kindergarten (often starting at age 3), elementary, secondary, and university. There are important differences between Japanese and western-style schools. Virtually every Japanese student studies the English language from Grade 7 throughout his or her final year of high school. All students and teachers clean their own classrooms and school buildings. Students are also required to memorize large numbers of facts.

Despite academic successes, impressive testing performances, and a literacy rate of 99 percent (the world's highest), educational reforms are presently being implemented to better prepare Japanese students for the future. One change being introduced is the use of task-oriented, individualized approaches to creative problem solving. Decreasing emphasis on the massive quantities of memorization is another change for Japanese students. Many Japanese feel the entrance exams required for high schools and universities are too stressful and the curriculum too rigid. Students believe that schools need to change in order to produce more creative and flexible citizens for the 21st century.

LEISURE TIME

Today, the Japanese are devoting more attention to leisure time than in the past. Reading, going out to eat, performing *karaoke* with friends, and traveling within Japan to hot springs and beaches are high on the list of leisure activities.

Riding on a train in Japan, you will probably observe the Japanese population doing one of two things—sleeping (due to demands of school and work) or reading. If they are reading, there is a significant chance they will be enjoying *manga*, a form of Japanese comic book. *Manga* are written for all ages of people with a wide, wide range of topics. Approximately 40 percent of all printed items in Japan are in this comic format. A popular leisure activity, *manga* offer an inexpensive form of entertainment. Moreover, *manga* are also used to introduce subjects such as history, law, or economics. They may be used as company brochures, for advertising, or for highlighting specific hobbies such as golf or soccer. The *manga* industry continues to find inviting ways to keep children and adults interested in this form of entertainment. Visual effects bring the reader into the story much like movies, yet are far cheaper to produce. With golfing fees of $150 or movie tickets of $20, *manga* offers affordable enjoyment for many people.

Renting a *karaoke* room with friends is a popular recreational activity amongst Japanese youth. Complete with microphones, a television screen, soft lighting, and low couch-style seating, these small rooms provide hours of fun for singing the lyrics to your favorite songs!

> *The sumo hero*
> *gently wades through an ocean*
> *of admirers.*
>
> Takai Kito (1741–1789)

By the time this *haiku* (a three-line poem consisting of a 5-7-5 syllable pattern) was written in the 18th century, *sumo* (Japanese wrestling) had become a popular spectator sport. *Sumo* began not as a sport, but as a religious event associated with the autumn harvest. Tradition tells that *sumo* wrestlers from farming villages divided into two groups to wrestle. The winning side held the belief that they had been favored by the gods and would have a better harvest because of this favor. Today, *sumo* tournaments are held 6 times per year, with each tournament lasting 15 days. Special rituals, such as throwing salt into the wrestling ring as a sign of purification, are performed each day of the tournament.

Baseball is another highly popular sport in Japan. Nearly every day of the baseball season, spectators cheer enthusiastically for their favorite teams! A major sporting event that occurs twice during baseball season is the national high school baseball tournament. Sports fans from all over Japan come to Koshien Stadium in Hyogo Prefecture to cheer for their team. The energy and enthusiasm produced by this event is phenomenal. Each team performs a number of rituals, such as attending shrines to pray and offering humble bows of thanks for a productive practice session. These rituals are done in hope of ensuring their team has done all it can to achieve success in the tournament.

There are many festivals and carnival celebrations in the Japanese year.
This crowd of worshippers is at a temple during the Sanji Festival in Tokyo.

ART FORMS AND CELEBRATIONS

A blend of traditional and contemporary culture can be found in Japanese celebrations. Art forms such as *chanoyu* (tea ceremony), *ikebana* (flower arranging), and *kabuki* (live theatrical performances) offer traditional rituals learned and performed in Japan.

Chanoyu dates back hundreds of years to rituals of

Buddhist monks. This ceremony, involving a series of steps to turn powdered green tea into a soothing hot beverage, was performed as a means of simplicity and concentration during the monks' meditations. *Ikebana* was used as a way to honor Buddhist and Shinto spirits. This unique skill of arranging flowers according to strict rules offers representations of heaven, earth, and people. The colorful staging of *kabuki* is filled with brilliant costuming, dramatic action, and expressive facial make-up. All character roles, whether portraying men or women, are played by men as ordered by tradition.

Contemporary customs and celebrations are especially evident in the lives of Japanese youth. Along with the popularity of *manga* and *karaoke*, animation has been popular in movies and television programming. Not only is this animation popular in Japan, but this concept is also reaching audiences worldwide.

Countless festivals and holiday celebrations are held in Japan throughout the year. Some are celebrated in local areas only, while others are popular across the entire country. Japan's most important holiday celebration is *oshogatsu*, the New Year. Companies and government offices are closed for the first 3 days of the year. The New Year is a time of togetherness for relatives. The holiday closing of schools and businesses allow families to travel by train, car, and air to gather for celebrations. Celebrations actually begin on New Year's Eve, when many Japanese families eat *soba* noodles as a representation and hope for a long life. Many also go to a local shrine or temple to pray for good fortune in the coming year. On New Year's Day, special foods and games are shared with family members and gifts of money are given to children. These activities are all done with the hopes of bringing health and happiness to the New Year.

An important summer festival in Japan is *Obon,* or Festival of the Dead. *Obon* festivities begin on August 13th and continue for 3 days. Buddhist in origin, this festival honors the spirit and memory of family ancestors. It is believed that the souls of the dead return home at this time of year. Thus, homes and gravestones are carefully cleaned. Special offerings of food are placed before the family altar in homes. Small fires or lanterns are set out to guide the souls of the dead to and from their homes. In some locations, people release paper lanterns to float on rivers, guiding the souls of the departed.

Children's festivals are widely celebrated in Japan as well. On March 3rd, a Doll Festival is held for young girls to wish for growth and good health. Children's Day for young boys, held on May 5th, is a day to wish for strength and health. *Tanabata,* the Star Festival, occurs on July 7th. On this day, children write wishes on colored strips of paper and tie them to bamboo branches. *Shichigosan,* or 'Seven-five-three' is celebrated on November 15th. On this day, 7-year-old girls, 5-year-old boys, and all 3-year-olds dress in kimonos and traditional clothing. The children then go to shrines with their parents to pray for continued health and growth. (Historically, these ages were milestone birthdays for having survived or overcome childhood diseases.)

Agricultural, seasonal, and local festivals are also celebrated throughout the country's landscape. No matter where one lives in Japan, a colorful event is sure to be celebrated with great honor and spirit!

A PEOPLE AND A PROVERB

"The nail that sticks up will get hammered down." What does this Japanese proverb mean to you? Japan is traditionally a group-oriented society in which no one individual wants to stand out. To do so shows great disrespect and dishonor. Loyalty and devotion to the group is valued and expected. This dedication reaches across all age groups, even to members of a baseball team.

Many Japanese traditions remain a strong part of society.

Yet, the younger generations are beginning to question some of these traditions, viewing them as needing reform. Family relations, roles of males and females, and career options are challenging the groupthink of Japanese society. What will these changes in social cohesion bring to Japan's future?

Japanese kindergarten children pose for the camera. The next generation of Japanese leaders will face many challenges, including how to maintain economic prosperity.

Japan
Looks Ahead

In your tour of Japan through the pages of this book you have learned about Japan's land, history, and people. You have seen how people in the Land of the Rising Sun have overcome countless hardships and obstacles to become a leading world economic power. Less than 150 years ago, they emerged from a shell in which they had taken refuge for over 300 years. In under a half-century, having undergone the many changes introduced during the Meiji Restoration, the small country became a major world power. During your reading, you have come to know the Japanese as a resilient, educated, hard-working, and honest people. They offer a great deal to admire and to respect. Japan has a literacy rate near 100 percent and the world's longest life expectancy. Indeed, a majority of Japanese believe that their lives are good.

As the world's most hazard-prone country, Japan will certainly continue to suffer the ravages of nature. Earthquakes will continue to cause massive destruction, accompanied by loss of both property and human lives. Seismic events will continue to create tsunamis that can wash entire communities off the map. Typhoons will continue to strike the islands, bringing howling winds, drenching rain, and accompanying disastrous flooding and landslides. Over the centuries, however, the Japanese have become accustomed to these hazards. Through wise planning, zoning, and building the potential for devastating losses is minimized.

Japan, with its 127 million people, is among the world's most densely crowded countries. The Tokyo-Yokohama metropolitan area alone has more people than the combined population of all states west of the Mississippi River except California and Texas. Rather than being a liability, however, Japan's people are its primary resource. A number of school reforms have been implemented that are designed to further improve the education of Japanese youngsters. This will surely make the country's human resources even more valuable in the future. So, too, will the continued rapid integration of women into a previously male-dominated society and workplace.

With a rate of natural population increase approaching zero percent, Japan's population is rapidly aging. Providing medical care, retirement pensions, and other needs of the elderly will place a huge strain on the country's already stressed economy. Who will fill the many jobs vacated by retirees? This is a matter of great concern to many Japanese. Currently, more than 99 percent of the people share a common race, culture, heritage, and values. Almost certainly, Japan will have to turn to foreign lands—China, South Korea, the Philippines, and else-where—to fill the labor gap. Many Japanese feel threatened by these changes. They worry about what will become of the way of life they have enjoyed and protected for so many centuries.

One gigantic question looming over Japan's future is its government. For nearly all of the past half century, the country has been ruled by the Liberal Democratic Party (LDP). Its future remains in doubt. Certainly, if Japan is to once again prosper, major changes need to be made in the way the country is governed. There is desperate need for new names and faces, new ideas and strategies. The LDP led the country through 40 years of booming economic growth and rapid social change. Today, however, many Japanese believe that their government is a bloated and corrupt bureaucracy. They attribute much of their country's woes to the very close (and often dishonest) relationship between government, banking, and business. They feel that their government is either unable or unwilling to make those hard decisions that are essential to improve the country's future.

Japan's economy, despite its present plunge, has many strengths on which to base recovery. It is a world leader in manufacturing a huge variety of products. Japanese products have a worldwide reputation for high quality and reasonable cost. The Japanese sales force may be the world's most effective. In many respects the country's current economic difficulties represent a relative, rather than absolute, hardship. According to the United Nations, there are 191 independent countries—189 of which rank *below* Japan economically! Most Japanese remain optimistic about their country's future. It would be premature to suggest that the sun is finally setting on the "Miracle of Japan." A country so accustomed to overcoming past obstacles certainly will survive its present crisis. The Land of the Rising Sun shall continue to shine brightly on the stage of modern world nations well into the future.

Facts at a Glance

Name	Japan
Official Name	Nippon or Nihon
Official Language	Japanese
Capital	Tokyo
Land Area	145,862 square miles (377,781 square kilometers)
Highest Elevation	Mount Fuji, 12,388 feet (3,776 meters)
Climate	Tropical and subtropical in the south; cool temperate in the north
Population	126,975,000 (2002 estimate)
Life Expectancy	81 years
Infant Mortality	3.8 deaths per 1,000 births
Ethnic Groups	99 percent Japanese, 1 percent Korean, Chinese, Brazilian, Filipino, and other
Religions	84 percent observe both Shinto and Buddhist, 16 percent other
Literacy	99 percent
Government	Constitutional monarchy with a parliamentary government
Independence	660 B.C. (Traditional founding by Emperor Jimmu)
Currency	Yen
Gross Domestic Product	$3.45 trillion (2002 estimate)
Unemployment	5 percent
Exports	Motor vehicles, semiconductors, office machinery, chemicals
Imports	Fuel, foodstuffs, machinery; textiles

30,000 B.C.	Japan's first settlers arrive.
10,000	The Jomon, a hunting and gathering people, settle Japan.
300	Yayoi people replace the Jomon and introduce agriculture.
300 A.D.-710 A.D.	The Kofun era. Chinese written language is introduced and the Yamato clan rises to power.
710-794	The Nara era. Japan's rulers build the country's first capital and begin to coin money and collect taxes.
794	Japan's rulers move the capital from Nara to Heian (present-day Kyoto).
1185	Minamoto clan defeats the Taira clan.
1192	Minamoto Yoritomo becomes the first shogun.
1274-1281	The Mongols under Kublai Khan try and fail to invade Japan.
1467-1477	Onin Wars devastate Kyoto.
1543	Portuguese traders arrive, bringing commerce, guns, and Christianity
1603	Tokugawa Ieyasu seizes control and moves capital to Edo (present-day Tokyo).
1640	Japan closes its doors to the rest of the world.
1853	U.S. Commodore Matthew C. Perry arrives in Tokyo Harbor and gains trading rights with Japan.
1867	The emperor is restored to power in the Meiji Restoration.
1894	Japan goes to war against China.
1904	Japan goes to war against Russia.
1910	Japan annexes Korea.
1923	The Great Tokyo earthquake kills thousands.
1926	Emperor Hirohito takes power.
1931	Japan seizes Manchuria.
1937	Japan wages a brutal war on China.
1941	Japan enters World War II against the United States and the Allies.
1945	Japan surrenders after the United States drops atomic bombs on Hiroshima and Nagasaki.
1952	The United States ends its occupation of Japan.

History at a Glance

1956   Japan becomes a member of the United Nations.

1964   Tokyo hosts Summer Olympics.

1972   Sapporo hosts the Winter Olympics.

1995   An earthquake devastates Kobe and Osaka.

1998   Nagano hosts the Winter Olympics.

Beasley, W.G. *The Japanese Experience.* Los Angeles, California: University of California Press, 2000.

Bix, Herbert P. *Hirohito and the Making of Modern Japan.* New York: Perennial, 2000.

Collinwood, Dean W. *Global Studies: Japan and the Pacific Rim* (Sixth Edition). Guilford, CT: Dushkin, 2001.

Ellington, Lucien. *Japan: A Global Studies Handbook.* Santa Barbara, CA: ABC-CLIO, 2002.

Gordon, Andrew. *A Modern History of Japan – From Tokugawa Times to the Present.* New York: Oxford University Press, 2003.

Japan. Baedeker Travel Guide. New York: Macmillan Travel, Simon & Schuster Macmillan, (published annually).

Shelley, Rex, T. C. Yong, and R. Mok. *Cultures of the World: Japan.* Singapore: Times Books International, 2002.

Whyte, Harlinah. *Countries of the World: Japan.* Singapore: Times Books International, 2002.

Websites

Central Intelligence Agency. *CIA-The World Factbook, Japan,* (annual update) *www.cia.gov/cia/publications/factbook* (Japan)

Geography Home Page. (General information on a variety of topics) *www.geography.about.com*

Japanese Government, Ministry of Foreign Affairs. Japan Information Network *www.jinjapan.org*

Library of Congress Country Studies: *Japan* *http://memory.loc.gov/frd/cs/jptoc.html*

National Clearing House for U.S./Japan Studies *www.indiana.edu/~japan*

Schauwecker's Guide to Japan *www.japan-guide.com*

U.S. Department of State: *Japan* *www.state.gov/countries*

Index

Index

Index

page:

About the Author

CHARLES F. "FRITZ" GRITZNER is Distinguished Professor of Geography at South Dakota State University in Brookings. He is now in his fifth decade of college teaching, research, and writing. In addition to his teaching, he enjoys traveling, writing, working with teachers, and sharing his love for geography with students and other readers. As consulting editor for the MODERN WORLD NATIONS series, he has a wonderful opportunity to combine each of these "hobbies." Gritzner has visited Japan on two occasions, most recently as a Great Plains-Rocky Mountain Region Japan Fellow. Dr. Gritzner has served as both president and executive director of the National Council for Geographic Education. He has received numerous awards in recognition of his achievements, including the NCGE's George J. Miller Award for Distinguished Service.

DOUGLAS A. PHILLIPS is an educator and writer who has traveled in over 70 countries. His many visits to Japan include travel as a Keizai Koho Center Fellow. During his career, Phillips has worked as a middle school teacher, a curriculum developer, a writer, and as a trainer of educators in various locations around the world. He has served as president of the National Council for Geographic Education and has received the Outstanding Service Award from the National Council for the Social Studies and numerous other awards recognizing his contributions to geography and social studies education. He, his wife Marlene, and their three children, Chris, Angela, and Daniel have lived in South Dakota and Alaska, but he and his family now reside in Arizona, where he writes and serves as an educational consultant.

KRISTI L. DESAULNIERS enjoys incorporating her travel experiences with students' learning. Ms. Desaulniers is an elementary school teacher with a Master's Degree in geography. Her love for travel has taken her to teaching assignments in England, Switzerland, Canada, and her home state of South Dakota. Other travels include a Keizai Koho Center Fellowship during which she had a wonderful opportunity to see and experience Japan and its culture. Ms. Desaulniers also has taught in Canada on a Fulbright Exchange and has received several teaching recognitions, including the Distinguished Teaching Achievement Award from the National Council for Geographic Education. She currently resides in Sioux Falls, South Dakota with her husband, Rob, in a home with memories, mementoes, and maps of travels to Japan and elsewhere.